IMAGES
of America

BAYONNE

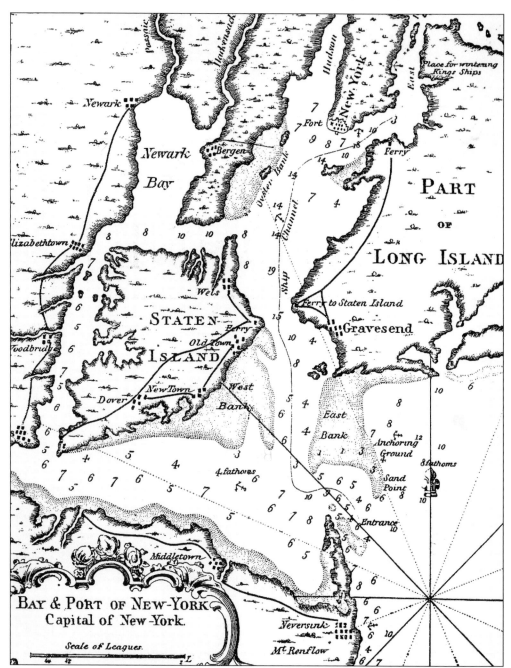

S. Bellin's map of New York Bay, 1764. The 3-mile long peninsula that forms Bayonne appears at the center of this navigational map, just below the small village of "Bergen" (see p. 7). The numbers throughout the map helped sailors avoid shallow water by showing the depth of the bay in fathoms (one fathom equals six feet). The "Oyster Banks" marked along Bayonne's eastern shore provided food for the Dutch immigrants who began settling the area after Henry Hudson explored New York Bay for the Dutch in 1609. Since then, countless immigrants have come to agree with Hudson that the bay is "a very good harbour for all windes." (Harvey, *Geneological History of Hudson and Bergen Counties, New Jersey* (1900))

IMAGES
of America

BAYONNE

By
Kathleen M. Middleton

ARCADIA

First published 1995
Second printing 1995
Copyright © Kathleen M. Middleton, 1995

ISBN 0-7524-0069-X

Published by Arcadia Publishing,
an imprint of the Chalford Publishing Corporation
One Washington Center, Dover, New Hampshire 03820
Printed in Great Britain

Cover photograph: The cover shows a crowd on 22nd Street during the Standard Oil Strike of 1915 (see p. 118). The "Day and Night Quick Lunch" car on the back cover was opened in 1913 by the father of America's fast-food industry, Jerry O' Mahoney. As Jerry realized, the shift workers on the Hook had such odd hours that they often missed meals. By putting a restaurant in a car that he could pull around town with horses, Jerry solved their problem by bringing meals right to the gates of the plants. The workers could then enjoy a hot meal at Jerry's counter "day or night" and still return to work before their fifteen-minute breaks ended (see p. 124). Jerry later created the first diner in America by turning one of these cars into a standing restaurant. (Newark Public Library)

Contents

To
Joseph McGlynn
and
Galileo Crisonino

A great city is that which has the
greatest men and women
—Walt Whitman

Popple's map of New York Bay, 1733. Bayonne lies around the area marked "Bergem Neck" at the center of this map. In 1733, Bayonne was still part of Bergen Township, which organized just three years after Petrus Stuyvesant bought the area from the Hackensack Indians in 1658. The Dutch began calling Bayonne's southeastern shore "Constable's Hook" after the Dutch West India Company gave the land to its chief gunner or "konstapel" in 1646. Bayonne remained part of Bergen Township until 1861 when it became a separate township. In 1869, Bayonne reorganized as a city. (Harvey, *Geneological History*)

Introduction

As the photographs on these pages show, the city of Bayonne, New Jersey, has made a number of significant contributions to American culture: from the country's first "rock band" and its first independent movie studio, to its first air-mail delivery and fast-food restaurants. This visual history of Bayonne brings these little-known contributions to light while focusing on the everyday lives of people in the City.

By looking at these photographs, we can gain a sense of what it was like to live in Bayonne between 1860 and 1940, the period in which Bayonne transformed itself from the "Newport on the Hudson" into the "Peninsula of Industry." These photographs trace the circumstances surrounding this transformation, as well as documenting its effects on day-to-day life. To a great extent, the experiences of Bayonne's residents during these years mirrored those of people throughout the country as the United States shifted from a rural to an industrial nation.

Yet even as these photographs allow us to rediscover the past, they also offer us a way to learn about ourselves: exploring the lives of the people in these photographs will help us understand our own.

Kathleen M. Middleton
March 1995

Acknowledgments

Like most people unfortunate enough not to have been born in Bayonne, my first view of it was from a car on the New Jersey Turnpike. Sixteen years ago, though, I had the good luck to become friends with Joe McGlynn, a Bayonne native. Joe not only shared his stories of Bayonne with me, but also introduced me to his friends in Bayonne: Bill Cleary, Bob Egan, Phil Falco, Mike Fedor, Kevin Glynn, Steve Jamolawicz, Julius Kiczek, Scott Lavender, Ernie Lettieri, John Mink, Fran Regan, and Tom Visone. Best of all, Joe introduced me to my husband, Edward J. Crisonino, another Bayonne native attending Rutgers College with us. Like five other Rutgers students—Barbara Bowley, Dave Brenner, Dan Krasner, Bruno Oriti, and Glenn Siegel—I soon became an honorary Bayonnite.

As I researched these photographs, the new Bayonne Historical Society was an enormous help. I am extremely grateful to P. Gerard Nowicki, the Society's publicist, who not only loaned me photographs, but also guided me through the collection at the Free Public Library and Cultural Center of Bayonne. Over the past year, he has patiently answered my questions and offered advice. Several members of the Society lent me photographs for the book: Lee and Barbara Fahley, Bill James, Carmela Karnoutsos, William Kowalski, Jonathan O'Donnell, and A. Resnick. Sneh Bains and her fine staff at the library, especially JoAnne Corbett, Dipali Sen, George Durman, and Richard Vanderburg, were helpful throughout my research. Thanks go also to the staffs of the Mercer County Library System and the Staten Island Historical Society.

A number of other Bayonnites shared their stories and photographs with me as I prepared this book. Ed's parents, Galileo and Florence Crisonino, kept me entertained with their wonderful stories, as did Tina Mills and Anselmo Crisonino. Joe's mother Marion and his sister Mary Rose Dokus lent me a number of photographs. Captain Bob Ramsay kindly shared his knowledge of the sea with me. Tony Troy, the playwright, also offered support. Mrs. C.L. Vreeland loaned me a number of photographs from her family album, and Doris Cash shared several pictures of St. Vincent's and the schools with me. R. Capriola, Michael K. Kostelnik, James Madden, and Joseph Wigdor all allowed me to publish several early photographs from their collections. Thanks also go to photographer Carl R. Hoetzl.

I must thank Lieutenant Peter Gwiazdowski for the history of the fire department and his delightful tour of Bayonne's Fire Museum—one of Bayonne's historical treasures. At the police department, Captain M. Rooney answered a number of questions while explaining the history of the force. Kathleen V. McKeand and John Bauer from Bayonne Hospital provided me with several pictures of the hospital and the Story family, while Rosemary Solan and Clare McLean provided me with pictures of Maidenform and the Rosenthals. The Board of the YMCA and Julia Wisniewski also shared photographs. Mrs. Pat Lee at St. Andrew's Church helped me identify several photographs.

Marc Wanamaker of the Bison Archives, Bebe Bergston of the Nieber Collection, and Paul Spehr of the Library of Congress graciously allowed me to use their rare photographs of David Horsley's Centaur Film Company. The New-York Historical Society, the Hagley Museum, the Jersey City Public Library, and the Newark Public Library were also kind enough to lend photographs for the book.

Finally, I must thank the anonymous reporters for *The Bayonne Herald*, whose stories provided many of the quotations in the book.

Author's Note: I have used the modern names for Bayonne's streets (shown on p. 115), rather than the original names (shown on pp. 20 and 21). The abbreviations "E." and "W." show whether the streets run east or west from Broadway. I have maintained the original spelling and punctuation of all cited texts, except where noted in brackets.

One
Newport on the Hudson
1860–1885

Schooner on the Kill, c. 1880. Staten Island appears in the background. This boy rows near a schooner in the Kill Van Kull, a body of water that flows around Bayonne's southern shore to link New York Bay with Newark Bay (see p. 20). Even in 1880, the shores of the Kill were still the Arcadia that the sailors on Henry Hudson's *Half-Moon* described in 1609: "pleasant with grass and flowers, and goodly trees, as ever they had seen." (Bayonne Public Library)

Welcome, 1860. This intricately-patterned gate opens to welcome the viewer up the gravelled drive of one of the many mansions that lined Avenue A during the nineteenth century. From "Daly's Point" opposite the Bergen Point Lighthouse (see p. 68), these mansions stretched north past George B. Spearin Jr.'s Crow's Nest at 8th Street, J.B. Close's estate at 19th Street, all the way to the Currie property at 52nd Street. The columns flanking the entrance gate are in the Italianate style, as is the mansion in the background. The cupola or lookout tower at the top of the mansion would have provided a wonderful view of Newark Bay. (M.K. Kostelnik)

An afternoon stroll, 1860. These gardens formed part of the Martin R. Cook estate on Avenue A opposite 8th Street. Martin was a successful New York merchant who commuted from Bayonne to his Manhattan office every morning on a steamboat like the one pictured on the opposite page. The people posed around the circular flower bed in the center could be members of the Cook family. The woman on the left wears a skirt with a short train over an oval-shaped hoop, the height of fashion in the early 1860s. Like the young ladies, she wears a summer bonnet to protect her delicate complexion. The man on the right is fashionably dressed in his high-buttoned suit and tall, rounded bowler hat. (M.K. Kostelnik)

Going to church, 1860. These people were identified in 1915 as a family leaving their home for church on Sunday. The two young ladies wait patiently in their crinolines, bonnets, and boots, while their brother, the young gentleman in the center, gets into the carriage. The man in the carriage holding the reins is probably the children's father. Although church was a short walk away, most families drove to it in their carriages to keep their clothing from being ruined in the muddy streets. After church, the family might have enjoyed a drive along the Kill Van Kull or up Avenue A. If it rained, they could have rolled down the curtains on the side of the carriage. (M.K. Kostelnik)

The Kill Van Kull, 1860. This view of the Kill from the roof of the La Tourette Hotel (see p. 14) shows a schooner sailing in the distance near the Staten Island shore. In the foreground, the sidewheeler *Thomas P. Way* stands moored at the dock in front of the La Tourette Hotel, where it stopped on Sundays to pick up passengers who wished to go to Newark or Manhattan. Passengers would board the boat just to the right, or "aft," of the paddle wheel. Once aboard, they could enjoy all the comforts of a twentieth-century ocean liner; sidewheelers had decks, private staterooms, dining rooms, saloons, and even ballrooms. (M.K. Kostelnik)

Bon Sejour, c. 1880. Mrs. Mary Belin DuPont preserved this photograph of the DuPont family's first home in America on the southeast corner of 1st Street and Broadway. The DuPonts came to Bayonne in 1800 after being persecuted by the French government during one of the tumultuous political upheavals that followed the French Revolution. In 1797, the French government not only arrested Pierre Samuel du Pont de Nemours, the family patriarch, but also seized the family's newspaper. Upon Pierre' release, the family sailed for America and settled in Bayonne. Pierre purchased this Dutch Colonial house and named it "Bon Sejour," or "Good Stay." When Pierre returned to France in 1802 to help Thomas Jefferson plan the Louisiana Purchase, his son Victor moved his family from Manhattan to Bon Sejour. In her memoirs, Victor's wife Gabrielle described it as a "cheerful house . . . very prettily situated" in a "healthful climate" with a "superb view" of the Kill. She also mentioned that Victor enjoyed Bayonne's "abundant fishing and hunting." After the DuPonts moved from Bayonne to Delaware in 1805, they first leased Bon Sejour to General Jean Victor Moreau, an exiled French officer, and then sold it in 1807. Maria Mullaney eventually inherited the property from her father, Elias Burger, and built a second house, the Mullaney Mansion, between Bon Sejour and the Kill. When Captain David La Tourette (see opposite) bought the 12-acre property in 1845 for $7,428, he turned the Mullaney Mansion into a two hundred-room hotel and used Bon Sejour to house servants (see p. 14). This photograph shows how Bon Sejour looked after the hotel opened. The vine-covered porch shown above was torn down around 1885. (Hagley Museum and Library)

Bon Sejour, c. 1880. The dog on the front porch seems too tired to lift his head for this photograph. Daniel Smith, a ferryboat captain, built the main part of this building around 1760. After the DuPonts moved here in 1800, they added this side wing (left) for use as a kitchen. They built another wing on the other side of the house for use as a dining room (see opposite). As they would in Delaware, the DuPonts decorated the rooms with fine furnishings and planted boxwood down their front walk. (Hagley Museum and Library)

Captain David La Tourette (1814–1891), c. 1865. With his goatee and moustache, David looks every bit the successful sea captain. A Bayonne native, he began sailing on his father's ships while still a young man. His father, the elder Captain David (1787–1865), made a fortune in shipping by running packet boats between Bayonne and southern cities such as Charleston and Savannah. In the 1840s he began using his fortune to develop a hotel and ferry in Bayonne (see pp. 12 and 14). The younger David continued to captain his father's ships until the end of the Civil War. During the war, he commanded the ship that brought supplies to General George B. McClellan's army when it was entrenched on the James River below Richmond in 1861. After the war, the younger David retired from the sea. His turn-down collar, knotted tie, and stickpin were popular post-Civil War men's fashions. (Bayonne Public Library)

An 1860 lithograph of the La Tourette Hotel. This view of the hotel from the Kill was drawn and lithographed by New York artist George Hayward. He probably drew it before April 24, 1860, the day that the *Red Jacket* (right) burned to the waterline while docked in Elizabeth. The hotel helped establish Bayonne's reputation as the "Newport on the Hudson," for it brought celebrities from around the country to the city. In 1881, Vice-President Chester A. Arthur stayed at the hotel; local tradition holds that President Ulysses S. Grant and Mark Twain also stayed here. Advertisements promoted the hotel's location as "one of the most healthy in the Country," with "good bathing, boating, and fishing." An 1881 article in the *New York Daily Graphic* recommends vacationing in "rural" Bayonne, home to "some of the best educated and most cultured families of the East." As the article notes, if guests tired of strolling on the grounds or driving in their carriages, a ferryboat could take them to Manhattan in just thirty-five minutes. Captain La Tourette also ran another ferry, the *Harlequin*, across the Kill to Staten Island. The pilot of the *Harlequin*, John MacDonald (b. 1824), explained that when it began running in the 1840s it held three horses and wagons, plus "as many passengers as could wedge themselves aboard. There was no shelter at all, and if it rained everybody got doused." Since the boat had no regular time table, "passengers on either side of the river used to signal us by hoisting a flag." John recalled that the "proper caper in those days for young folks was to hire the *Harlequin* for moonlight excursions up Newark Bay. Lots of times she would go as far as the lighthouse . . . [get stuck in Newark Bay's shallow waters, and] refuse to budge an inch further" (see p. 152). (Bayonne Historical Society)

Bird's-eye view, *c*. 1860. This view from the roof of the center portion of the La Tourette Hotel looks east toward Brooklyn and Staten Island, which appear in the distance at the end of New York Bay. The flagpole in the foreground stands atop the eastern wing of the hotel. The building just behind the trees to the left of the flagpole is the La Tourette Stables on Broadway, where guests at the hotel could rent horses and carriages for a drive along the Kill. To the right of the flagpole, a cupola with scalloped trim tops Rufus Story's mansion, which appears on the far right of the lithograph on the opposite page. Rufus built this mansion on the northeast corner of Broadway and 1st Street soon after he moved to Bayonne in 1845 (see p. 26). He bought the hotel across the street from Captain La Tourette's heirs in 1883. Moving down 1st Street toward Brooklyn, the next building was the home of Albert M. (d. 1874) and Anne La Tourette Zabriskie. Albert's family, descendants of the last king of Poland, had settled at Bergen Point in the eighteenth century. After attending college, Albert became a farmer and married Captain La Tourette's daughter, Anne. By 1848, they had left his family's farm to manage her father's hotel. They moved into this home at the corner of Lord Avenue and 1st Street when Albert retired in 1855; Albert lived here when he became Bayonne's first county freeholder in 1860. Further down 1st Street past the Zabriskie's home appear L.L. and Martha Spring's mansion, Colonel Charles W. Fuller's mansion, the Vesey home, and the the Smith home. This view of the Kill changed dramatically in 1865 when the Central Railroad Company built a 2,650-foot wharf, Port Johnston, on the Kill just east of 1st Street (see p. 20). (New York Historical Society)

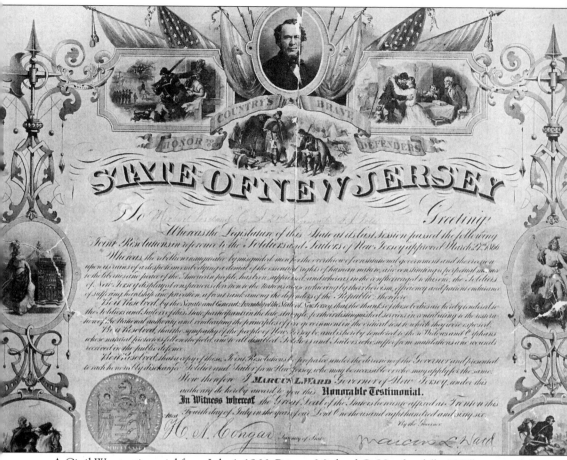

A Civil War testimonial from July 4, 1866. Private Michael G. Vreeland (b. 1835) received this certificate for serving in Company I of the 21st Infantry Regiment of the New Jersey Volunteers (see p. 39). In the document, New Jersey Governor Marcus L. Ward thanks Michael for helping to "suppress" the "rebellion" by "misguided men" to deny the "essential rights of human nature." After Southern soldiers began the Civil War by firing on Fort Sumter on April 12, 1861, over five-hundred men from Bayonne volunteered to fight the South. Some of the first men to enlist were from the Close Light Guards, a local militia that took the name of the wealthy Bayonne resident, Joseph Bailey Close, who paid for their uniforms and equipment. With other men from Bayonne, the Guards left Bayonne for Annapolis on May 3, 1861, under the command of Captain John J. Van Buskirk of Company E. Once John became a major, his cousin Captain Hiram Van Buskirk (1830–1886) commanded Company E. Meanwhile, another of John's cousins, Captain James Van Buskirk, almost died while imprisoned for six months in the South's notorious Andersonville Prison in Georgia. Between the diseases and the poor food at Andersonville, James dropped from 191 to 119 pounds. Even so, he considered himself lucky to have entered the prison at all. As he later explained, he was scouting near Port Walthall on the Appomattox River on May 22, 1864, when a North Virginia unit captured him. Within minutes, one of the Southern officers shouted "lets hang the d—d Yankee," and began tying a noose around a tree. Yet just as the Southerners finished tying the knot, Captain Jack Kennedy, their commander, appeared on the scene and persuaded them to imprison James rather than hang him. It seems that Jack and James were old friends, having met in 1859, when James sailed from Virginia to New York on the Captain's boat, the *Sherwood*. (C.L. Vreeland)

Adjutant Andrew C. Van Buskirk (1835–1901), *c.* 1861. Andrew received this sword and rifle when he enlisted on May 1, 1861, just one week after he married Adeline Williams. Andrew served in Company E under his brother Hiram, who had left a wife and two children to enlist (see opposite). Both men were born at the Van Buskirk homestead on Constable Hook (see p. 22). (James Madden)

An 1867 lithograph of a Saltersville murder. *Frank Leslie's Illustrated Weekly* published this picture of James Spencer (left) attacking three boys in a wagon as they rode through "Saltersville" in northern Bayonne on October 12, 1867 (see p. 38). According to *Leslie's*, James told the boys to "shut up your gab; if you don't, I'll shoot." After the boys continued to beg for their lives, the "young monster deliberately fired upon them," killing two of them. (New York Public Library)

Robbins' Reef Lighthouse from a c. 1870 lithograph. Long before the Statue of Liberty's torch lit New York Bay, this lighthouse led ships around the shallow waters over Robbins' Reef off Constable Hook (see p. 20). Lighthouse keepers lived here with their families, manning the light by night and sleeping during the day. Captain John Walker kept the light from 1882 until his death in 1886. Before he died, he told his wife to "Keep the light burning, Kate." She did. After manning the light each evening, she rowed her children, Jacob and Mary, ashore for school each morning. Whatsmore, by the time she retired in 1919, this 4-foot 10-inch woman had used her rowboat to rescue over fifty people from drowning. Kate, a German immigrant, had met John when her boat from Germany accidentally landed at Sandy Hook rather than Manhattan. (Bayonne Public Library)

An 1874 lithograph of a goats and geese round-up. Although by 1874 trains like the one on the left were rushing through Bayonne every half-hour, Bayonne was still a rural community with cows, pigs, and goats in most backyards. If these animals roamed loose, they became a nuisance by destroying property. Rufus Story, for instance, once complained that stray goats had ruined his trees by eating the bark off them (see p. 26). To protect property owners, the Bayonne Police rounded up strays and brought them to the city pound at the foot of E. 11th Street (see p. 23). To get the animals back, their owners had to go to the pound and pay the pound keeper $1 for each one. When *The Bayonne Herald* published this lithograph, it identified the officer on the far left as Police Chief George B. Whitney. The scene shows the entire police force pulling stray animals up Broadway past the Central Railroad building at the corner of Broadway and Cottage Street. The *Herald* reported several such round-ups in 1874. During one of them, patrolman James Russell impounded fifty-four goats in just a few hours. Stray goats caused trouble even in this century: in 1902, the *Herald* reported that thirteen "whiskered specimens of the capricornus buckibus" were caught grazing on the terraced lawn of Bayonne City Hall (see p. 43). According to the *Herald*, Janitor John J. Keating drove the goats away after he realized that "they were not politicians in disguise." (Bayonne Public Library)

An 1873 map of Bayonne. This map from *The Hudson County Atlas* misspells the "Kill Van Kull" as the "Kill Von Kull." The map does, however, show many of the original names of Bayonne's streets. In 1888, the city council decided to simplify the street names to receive free postal delivery. Following the Philadelphia plan of lettered avenues and numbered cross streets, the city council changed South Avenue to W. 7th Street, Summit to 20th, 16th to 22nd, and

so on (see p. 115). Bayonne's three wards were also known as Bergen Point (south), Centreville, and Pamrapo or Saltersville (see p. 38). Until the State built the New Jersey Turnpike over the Morris Canal, various businessmen proposed enlarging the Morris Canal into a ship canal, as the dotted lines show here. (Crisonino Family)

Henry Meigs (1809–1887), c. 1870. Soon after Henry and his wife Mary Noel Meigs (1811–1890) moved to Bayonne in the 1860s, they built a mansion on Newark Bay. Henry, the son of a New York congressman, had worked his way up from a job as an assistant cashier at a New York bank to a term as the president of the New York Stock Exchange. After being elected as Bayonne's first mayor in April 1869, Henry served as mayor for ten years. *The Bayonne Times* described him as an "honorable, high-minded gentleman of the old school." Henry's son Henry (1849–1903) seems to have been of the "new school." While serving as a city councilman in 1901, the younger Henry shocked the nation with his suggestion to prohibit women from wearing long skirts, because they picked up germs as they dragged on the ground. After women throughout the country protested the idea, Dr. Lucius Donohoe consoled Henry with the fact that ladies did not vote (see p. 55). When asked about the debate, Judge Hyman Lazarus simply noted that skirts should be "just over two feet" (see p. 43). (Bayonne Public Library)

The Van Buskirk homestead, c. 1885. For over two hundred years, members of the Van Buskirk family lived in this farmhouse, which faced east on the north shore of the Hook. At its peak, the farm's orchards "yielded fruit by the thousand barrels," according to Edward E. Van Buskirk (see p. 47). Although many Van Buskirk men fought for the North in the Civil War, Charles Winfield found an 1757 advertisement for the sale of "a parcel of likely negro slaves just arrived from Guinea" at this farm. (Bayonne Public Library)

The Bayonne Police, c. 1875. Bayonne's first police force had a variety of duties besides impounding stray animals (see p. 19). The 1870 *Police Rules and Regulation Manual* directed them to fine people driving their horses over 6 miles per hour, as well as anyone swimming within 400 yards of the city who was not "clothed from the neck and armpits to the knees." The police arrested only truly dangerous criminals, such as "loafers and bummers who are in the habit of hanging around street corners for the purpose of staring at or insulting ladies." After their arrest, criminals were held in cells at police headquarters, which was in the cellar of the building above, the new city hall at Broadway and 22nd Street (see p. 42). The City installed the gaslight on the left in October 1874, a few months after the building opened. The police force had grown quickly after the city council created it on September 21, 1869, with three full-time patrolmen: Thomas Connolly, Jack Van Pelt (b. 1830), and John D. Vreeland (b. 1832). Just one year later, the council named George B. Whitney as police chief and appointed four more patrolman. The members of the department shown above are, from left to right: Arthur Cavanaugh, Cornelius Van Horn, Michael Connolly, Chief George B. Whitney (1830–1901), Michael McNamara, Jack Van Pelt, Thomas Connolly, and John D. Vreeland. Mayor Henry Meigs (opposite) stands on the porch in the background. (Bayonne Police Department)

LIST
OF
ORIGINAL MEMBERS.

————◆◆◆————

V. T. Eddy, Jr.	E. Scofield.
C. C. Earl.	W. J. Lyon.
Geo. A. Lacas.	N. Stafford.
R. W. Besson.	Eugene Randall.
. H. Carragan.	Alex. Christie.
Emmet Smith.	B. F. Wilson.
W. L. Weston.	Geo. W. Yates.
Henry Burdett.	B. L. Coffin.
. Berry.	J. R. Cruikshank.
W. C. Post.	W. C. Hamilton.
A. McFarlan,	A. J. Ford.
Geo. H. Cadmus.	A. J. Van Buskirk.
. F. Dates.	J. T. B. Collins.
. L. Dowe.	

Hope Hook & Ladder Compan
No. 2,
OF THE CITY OF BAYONNE, N. J.

————◆◆◆————

ORGANIZED JANUARY 25, 1873
————◆◆◆————

Officers:

FOR THE YEAR ENDING JANUARY 25, 1874.

FOREMAN,	.	.	.	E. BERRY.
ASST. FOREMAN,	.	.	.	W. T. EDDY, Jr.
SECRETARY,	.	.	.	A. CHRISTIE.
TREASURER,	.	.	.	J. R. CRUIKSHANK
STEWARD,	.	.	.	GEO. A. LACAS.

Standing Committees.

————

COMMITTE OF FINANCE:

B. L. COFFIN,   N. STAFFORD

E. SCOFIELD.

INVESTIGATING COMMITTEE:

J. T. B. COLLINS,   E. C. EARL

The Hope Hook and Ladder Company manual of January 1874. When the twenty-seven men listed on the left formed the Hope Company in 1873, they named themselves after Colonel W.C. Hope, a Central Railroad Company official (see p. 44). The first Monday of every month they met in a red one-room schoolhouse at 193 Broadway in their uniforms: black firehats, blue flannel shirts, and black-glazed belts. Bayonne's first volunteer company, "Bayonne Hook and Ladder No. 1," wore similar uniforms, with red rather than blue shirts. These groups were called "hook and ladder companies," because their trucks were equipped with 3-gallon leather buckets hanging from hooks next to their ladders. For several years, they fought fires with nothing more than buckets and ladders. When the fire gong rang, they rushed to their headquarters to pull their trucks to the fire with tow ropes (see p. 66). Once at the fire, they would take their ladders and buckets off the truck and quickly form lines to pass the buckets from the nearest well to the fire, then back again. The firemen began using hoses in 1876 when the new "Independence Fire Association" bought the first hand-pumper truck in the City, fully equipped with 400 feet of canvas hose. The firemen still had to rely on wells for water, though, and if the well they were using ran dry, they had to stop fighting the fire to look for a new well. In June 1882 a dry well kept the firemen from stopping a fire in Patrick Peyton's blacksmith and wheelwright shop on Broadway. As the firemen raced from well to well looking for water, the fire spread to Joseph Anderson's house next door. The following month, the City solved the water problem by installing fire hydrants. (Bayonne Fire Department)

The Bergen Point-Port Richmond Ferry, c. 1875. Having bought their tickets in the ferryhouse (left), these people follow the delivery van up the ramp to board the ferryboat docked at the right. After the Bergen Point-Port Richmond Ferry Company built this dock on 1st Street in 1873, their ferries ran back-and-forth over the Kill every fifteen minutes from 6 am to 9 pm. The La Tourette Hotel can be seen faintly in the background over the trees. (Bayonne Public Library)

St. Mary's Church, c. 1880. In 1861, Reverend James Callan of Newark consecrated this building as the first Roman Catholic church in Bayonne. The area's small Catholic community had begun planning the church in 1852, when Reverend John Kelly celebrated the first Mass in the city at the home of John Welsh at 31 Lord Avenue. As Bayonne's population leapt from 1,700 in 1865 to 9,572 in 1880, the parish outgrew this church, and Father Thomas M. Killeen began building a new one on 14th Street and Avenue C.

Top: Rufus Story (1813–1887), *c.* 1875. Bottom: Ursula D. Ayres Story (1817–1891), 1880.

Posing in his wide collared jacket and cravat (or tie), Rufus looks thoughtfully at the camera, showing what the *Bayonne Times* called his "persistent and determined temperament." Ursula smiles sweetly under her dainty breakfast cap, a style married ladies wore throughout the nineteenth century. Horatio Alger could have used Rufus as one of the heroes in his "rags-to-riches" novels, for although Rufus began penniless, he accumulated over $6 million by the time of his death. He served as one of Bayonne's first councilmen, and even saved the City from bankruptcy by loaning it $75,000. Rufus started his climb at the age of fifteen, when he left his parents in Dutchess County, New York, to make his fortune in Manhattan. He began working as a clerk in a grocery store, saved his money, and bought the store just one year later. He soon shifted the business from selling groceries to trading in spices. By 1838, his spice trading business had grown so large that he bought a warehouse for it at 7 Front Street near Battery Park, where he ran the business for the next fifty years. According to one of his employees, he "paid close attention to business, and personally looked after every item on his books." Around 1845, he moved to Bayonne with his wife and two daughters. After the death of his first wife, he married Urusula, and they built a mansion on 1st Street (see p. 27) where they raised their two daughters, Alice and Abby (see opposite). (Bayonne Hospital)

Top: Alice Story Rowland (b. 1858), *c.* 1880.
Bottom: Abby Augusta Story Marshall
(b. 1860), *c.* 1880.

Like other young ladies in the nineteenth
century, Alice and Abby would not have been
allowed to wear their hair "up," coiled in
braids at the top of their heads as shown here,
until their eighteenth birthdays. Both girls
were popular members of Bayonne's
fashionable society. When their parents gave
Abby a party in June 1883, they hired the
steamboat *John Moore* to take her one hundred
guests up the East River to see the new
Brooklyn Bridge. After a two-hour boat ride,
the party returned to the Story mansion for
dinner and dancing in what *The Bayonne
Herald* described as their "large and brilliantly
lighted parlors." Soon after their father Rufus
died of a stroke in 1887, Alice and Abby
decided to build a hospital as a memorial to
him. Between illnesses in Bayonne's growing
population and injuries from Bayonne's new
industries (see p. 30), the city desperately
needed a hospital. With guidance from Solon
Humphreys (see p. 54), Alice and Abby built a
hospital on 30th Street, still in operation
today, and placed a plaque that read "In
memory of Rufus Story" over a terra-cotta and
oak fireplace in the rear hall (see p. 55). Their
mother helped them by spending $17,000 to
completely furnish the building with goods
such as iron beds, linen sheets, and feather
pillows for the patients' rooms. (Bayonne
Hospital)

The shore of Newark Bay, *c.* 1884. This lady and young gentleman rest on a log around 40th Street to enjoy the view of the bay and the Passaic Lighthouse (see p. 152). As industry began to fill the Hook in the 1870s, residents began turning to Bayonne's Newark Bay shore for recreation. The oak trees in back of them were part of the woods that filled Bayonne's upper west side and served as a movie set for Centaur Films (see p. 94). (Bayonne Public Library)

The Newark Bay shore, *c.* 1884. This detail from the picture above shows the three-quarter sleeves and bustled skirt that were popular women's styles in 1884. The bustle, a large, padded pouf at the back of a woman's skirt, disappeared in the 1860s, only to become stylish again around 1882. To create these bustles, women wore pads over specially-shaped hoop skirts beneath their dresses. Although these suits were called "walking costumes," walking anywhere in them must have been difficult, because they weighed nearly 10 pounds. (Bayonne Public Library)

Two
The Peninsula of Industry
1886–1899

Railroad Workers, *c.* 1890. During America's post-Civil War economic boom, the Jersey Central Railroad helped transform Bayonne into the "Peninsula of Industry" by providing industries with a cheap, quick way to bring raw materials such as coal, iron, and copper to their factories on Constable Hook (see p. 46). These workers pose with an engine on the tracks near 22nd Street (see p. 44). After the railroad laid tracks through Bayonne in 1864, so many Irish immigrants took jobs with the railroad and settled along E. 22nd Street on the Hook, that Bayonnites began calling the area "Irishtown." (Bayonne Public Library)

Left: John Henry Brower, Sr., *c.* 1885.

Right: Susan Evelyn Brower Harding (b. 1867), *c.* 1883.

After fighting in the Civil War, John moved his family from Staten Island to Bayonne, where he opened a store on 33rd Street. John's daughter Susan may have posed in this fashionable bustled dress for her wedding to Eugene D. Harding in 1881. Two years after their wedding, Eugene was killed by a train while working as a cooper for the Standard Oil Company (see opposite). An inquest into Eugene's death found Standard negligent for not hiring enough workers to run the train safely. The only man on the train, the brakeman, was too busy running the controls to see Eugene standing next to the track. A few months after Eugene's death, Susan gave birth to Eugene's only child (see p. 75). (Johnathon O'Donnell)

Michael Oleskie (1847–1933), *c.* 1890. Michael emigrated from Poznan, Poland, to Bayonne in 1873. At some point after arriving in Bayonne, he changed his name from "Olszewski" to "Oleskie." Like many immigrants in Bayonne at the time, Michael worked at the Standard Oil refinery. He seems to have been a model employee, for his superintendent recommended him as a "steady, sober" man who was "attentive to his duties." Within five years, he had saved enough money from his job to return to Poland to bring his wife, Marianna, and two sons to America. After Marianna's death, he remarried and moved to 197 Avenue F. While living here, he helped organize the Mount Carmel Roman Catholic Church for Bayonne's growing Polish population. (Bill James)

The Standard Oil Company from an 1885 lithograph. *Leslie's Magazine* published this view from the Staten Island shore of Standard's works on the Hook. As John MacDonald recalled (see p. 14), Standard "created the first really big boon for the city" when its owner, John D. Rockefeller, bought 176 acres on the Hook in 1872. Within a few years, Rockefeller gained control of 90 percent of America's oil industry, and Bayonne became a key piece of his empire. An 1881 *New York Herald* headline explained that for Bayonne, oil was the "Aladdin at Whose Bidding a City Rises." Indeed, by 1885, Rockefeller had built a small city on the Hook—forty stills, ten condensers, sixty tanks, and a barrel factory—where his employees refined products such as the famous "Standard White Oil" for kerosene lamps. The refining work began when crude oil arrived on the Hook. To purify it, the workers boiled it in stills. After funnelling the vapors from the boiling oil through a condenser and into a tank, they emptied the refined oil in the tanks into barrels for delivery around the world. Placing these works in Bayonne helped Rockefeller lower the costs of shipping oil. Since the refineries were next to the docks, he did not have to pay to ship barrels of refined oil to the coast by train, as he did with his refineries in Ohio. By 1885, he had also built pipelines to Bayonne from Texas to lower the cost of shipping crude oil to the Hook. Between 1875 and 1885, these pipelines enabled Rockefeller to slash the price of refined kerosene from 5¢ to less than 1¢ a gallon. Yet while the pipelines helped Standard cut costs, they also created many problems for Bayonne's fishermen. *The Bayonne Herald* soon complained that oil leaking from the pipes was driving the oysters from Newark Bay. In 1886 the *Herald* reported that the "sludge acid," the thick green residue that remained after boiling the crude oil, was killing fish and corroding boats. According to the *Herald*, the salt meadows near the refineries had become covered with the "offensive green slime" from the acid. Once it hardened, it made "a bed resembling the patent road invented by Mac Adam," which Standard was using as a foundation for additional refinery buildings. (Bayonne Library)

A Memorial Day parade, May, 31, 1886. After the Civil War ended in 1865, Americans began to celebrate Memorial Day by placing flowers on the graves of soldiers who died in the war. This picture shows Bayonne's first Memorial Day parade, which was organized by the veterans standing at the far left of the picture, members of the James N. Van Buskirk Post 100 of the Grand Army of the Republic. *The Bayonne Herald* reported that the weather for the parade was perfect: cloudy enough to "keep back the rays of the sun" with "wind enough to stir the bunting that was everywhere displayed." The parade began at 9:00 am in front of the veterans' headquarters at Wulf's Hall (see opposite). From here, the veterans marched to each school in Bayonne so that schoolchildren could give them flowers for the soldiers' graves. Leading the march were the "Castleton, Staten Island Citizens' Cornet Band" and the Bayonne drum corps standing in the middle of this picture. After city officials reviewed the parade in front of city hall, the carriages pictured above took the lead in the procession to the Van Buskirk Cemetery on the Hook. Some of the officials in the carriages are: Mayor David Oliver, Recorder J.H. Besher, Councilmen William C. Farr (see opposite), J.H. Sleaman, William J. O'Brien, and William Kelly. Four veterans also rode in the carriages: Henry Harris, George Atwater, Dr. Noah Sanborn, and Hiram Van Buskirk. Having decorated the graves at the cemetery, the parade then proceeded up Broadway to board a train for additional festivities in Jersey City. This picture was probably taken on the march back from the cemetery, because the *Herald* reported that the parade "halted once" at the end of the parade when "the muzzle of a deadly camera was brought to bear on them at close range" near the Reformed Dutch Protestant Church on Broadway (above), the first church in Bayonne. (Bayonne Public Library)

Charles G. Hendrickson, *c.* 1890. Charles was the popular owner of the "G. A. R. Assembly Rooms," or "Wulf's Hall," a saloon at 671 Broadway. After George Carragan constructed the building as a grocery store in the 1860s, the city council met on its second floor from 1869 to 1873. Peter Wulf converted the store into a saloon in 1878, then sold it to Charles in 1887. This portrait of Charles in his formal white tie could have been taken for his sister's wedding to A. Haldin at the hall on May 14, 1890. Charles, the best man, turned the hall into a "bower" of palms, ferns, and vines for the occasion, according to *The Bayonne Herald*. After the ceremony, the guests enjoyed supper at tables "decorated with bouquets of flowers, potted plants, and highly colored Japanese handkerchiefs," then danced until dawn to the music of Professor Edward G. Brown's orchestra. (R. Capriola)

William Charles Farr (b. 1844), *c.* 1890. After emigrating from Gettenbach, Germany, in 1861, William began working in Bayonne as a stone-cutter and wed Mary Dorethea Schmidt, another German immigrant. He soon bought a canal boat, which he used to ferry goods between Newark, Bayonne, and Jersey City. As canal traffic slowed in the 1870s (see p. 56), William decided to sell his boat and open a contracting business. Between building factories on the Hook and homes for Hook employees, his business flourished. He served as a city councilman for eight years and then became mayor in 1891. He was so popular after his first term as mayor that he ran unopposed in 1893, having received both the Democratic and Republican nominations. (Bayonne Public Library)

Baseball, c. 1887. The two boys in the center peep though the fence to see the members of the Bergen Point Athletic Club, who are in the field wearing their crimson shirts and white knickerbocker pants. The Pointers built this field on Broadway and 4th Street in 1884, when six balls made a walk and pitchers could still take a short run before throwing the ball. While playing on this field between 1884 and 1888, the Pointers became one of the most famous teams on the East Coast; the *Philadelphia Record* named them as one of the three best teams in the country. After they won the pennant of the Amateur Baseball League in 1886, their pitcher, Alonzo Stagg, turned down an offer to play professional baseball for $3,000 a season. Alonzo eventually gained national fame as the football coach at the University of Chicago. This picture probably dates from 1887, the year teams began replacing team benches with dugouts like the ones shown here. The Pointers often drew crowds of over 1,200 to their games that summer. Between innings, the young ladies in the stands sent boxes of chocolates to their favorite players. Now and then, the umpire or "judge" had to stop the game when a fog rolled in from the Kill. After the Pointers reorganized as the New Jersey Athletic Club in 1888, they began playing on a new field on Newark Bay. In 1898, they became part of the New York Knickerbockers. To capture this view of the field, the photographer stood on the roof of a building on Avenue C, looking towards Broadway across the vegetable gardens in what is today's Story Court. The Reformed Church on Lord Avenue appears in the background behind the trees at the center of the picture. Today, St. Andrew's Roman Catholic Church stands on this site (see p. 109). (Bayonne Public Library)

Bergen Point, 1892. This view looking east on 1st Street shows why people from Jersey City, Elizabeth, and Newark flocked to Bergen Point on warm summer evenings. Walking on gravel paths like the one on the right, they could enjoy the cool breezes from the Kill, as well as the beautiful view. After sunset, the view shifted to 1st Street, where, according to *The Bayonne Herald*, bicycle lights flickered like "fire-flys dashing hither and thither in the darkness." (Lee Fahley)

John H. MacDonald (b. 1844), c. 1895. The son of John and Hannah Everson MacDonald, John grew up on the Bergen Point Lighthouse where his father and then his mother served as keepers (see p. 68). Soon after Abraham Lincoln appointed John keeper, he left the light for the Civil War. After the war, he wed Ann L. Barnes of Staten Island and opened the Riverside House, a restaurant on 1st Street that quickly became popular with both residents and tourists. (Harvey, *Geneological History*)

McGiehan's boat works, *c.* 1894. Between 1850 and 1900, boat works like this one turned Bayonne's northern New York Bay shore into one of the finest yacht building centers in the country. Captain Patrick McGiehan (1823–1901) built this wooden shed for his boat works on New York Bay and 45th Street around 1840 after emigrating to Bayonne from Donegal, Ireland. In this shed, he built sloops like the *Meteor* and cat boats like the *Psyche*, as well as one of the first torpedo boats in the world. The man standing on the left is probably one of Patrick's three sons, who joined him in the business. Just two blocks south of McGiehan's at Odell's Cove was the shop of Bayonne's most famous yacht builder, Captain Robert Fish (1813–1883) (see p. 83). Fish gained international fame in 1852 when he designed and built the *Una* for Lord Coyngham of England. Further south at the foot of 35th Street, Captain Philip Elsworth designed prize-winning yachts such as the *Atlantin*, the *Comet*, and the *Penguin* (see opposite). Philip's brother, Captain Joseph Elsworth (1831–1902), made yachting history by piloting the *Puritan* to victory over the *Genesta* in the 1885 America's Cup Races. Bayonne celebrated the victory by giving Joseph a banquet at Schuyler Hall with ex-Mayor Henry Meigs presiding. By 1870, the Elsworth brothers had also started the "J.W. Elsworth Company," which sold the oysters that they raised in Newark Bay to local stores and restaurants. Once they began shipping oysters by train, their company grew rapidly, and by 1886, they were sending over 30,000 bushels of oysters a month to California alone. (Bayonne Public Library)

Captain Philip Elsworth (1828–1909), c. 1884. Having grown up on the sea aboard his father William's ships, Philip became captain of his own ship before he was even twenty years old. During the Civil War, his ship was the first to enter Savannah, Georgia, to bring supplies to General W.T. Sherman's troops after their famed "March to the Sea." When Philip sailed home from the war, one of his passengers was Robert Reddick, an ex-slave who had fought at Charleston. Once they landed in Bayonne, Philip wed Mrs. Lydia Willits Cramer and retired from the sea to raise a family (see p. 40), build yachts, and sell oysters. Robert found work at the Van Buskirk farm (Shaw, *History of Essex and Hudson Counties*).

The Salter house, c. 1894. When David Salter settled in Bayonne in 1832, he bought a farm that stretched from bay to bay and built this home on W. 48th Street from blocks of sandstone quarried near by. At the time, the northern part of Bayonne was called "Pamrapaugh," an Indian word meaning "land of wealth." As David began selling lots from his farm to men such as John Elderson, a wheelwright, and John Rowland, a blacksmith, people began calling the area "Saltersville" (or "Salterville," as it is occasionally spelled). (Bayonne Public Library)

Mullaney's grocery store, c. 1894. These children pose on the porch of the informal meeting center of Saltersville, a grocery store that Hess Sharret built around 1835 near today's 49th Street. The sign in the window behind them advertises "Quaker Oats." The store became "Mullaney's" around 1860 when an Irish immigrant named Owen Mullaney bought it. Until mail began to be delivered in 1889, everyone in Saltersville came here daily for their mail, groceries, and local news. (Bayonne Public Library)

The Vreeland family portrait, *c.* 1893. After Michael, a fisherman, returned from the Civil War (see p. 16), he married Joanna Van Buskirk (1846–1933). They pose here with their sons Frank (left) and Harry in the living room of their home on Newark Bay at 32nd Street (see p. 51). The heavy velvet curtains behind them, the floral wallpaper, and the Eastlake sofa were typical late nineteenth-century furnishings. (C.L. Vreeland)

Bathing houses, *c.* 1895. William Armbruster captured this view of the bathing houses (left) on Newark Bay around 40th Street. One Sunday in 1895, a *Bayonne Herald* reporter found many "pleasure seekers" lunching and bathing here, while a few blocks away, the Salvation Army held a service next to a shooting range. The reporter noted that although the Salvationists' prayers were "earnest," their music, accompanied by bass and kettle drums, was "very, very bad." (Bayonne Public Library)

School No. 6, 1890. When this class graduated, they created a stir by exhibiting outdated schoolbooks such as *Algebra, 1862* to convince the school board to buy new books. The graduates posing here with their teachers are Alida Conover, Jane M. Ramsay, Linna Small, Louise Bowman, Belle Cooney, Florence Cadmus, Josephine Davis, Frank Clark, and Philip Elsworth (see p. 69). Mr. E.C. Earl, standing on the far left, became the principal of this twelve-room school on W. 38th Street when it opened in December 1888. Mr. Earl began teaching in Bayonne in 1866 for $800 a year. (Bayonne Library)

School No. 1, *c.* 1890. This brick school on 5th Street opened in 1876. The boy standing in the snow at the left could be William H. Alpers, whose father sold this picture as a postcard in his drugstore at 202 Avenue D. William's father immigrated to Bayonne around 1865 after his trustees in Hamburg, Germany, had squandered his inheritance. He became a pharmacist and eventually owned several drugstores in Bayonne. (Bayonne Library)

The Till Rock Band, c. 1889. The Till family, the world's first rock band, became famous for the music of their "rockaphones," xylophone-like instruments made out of hornblende and schist rocks. When they arrived in Bayonne from Keswick, England, in 1885, they intended to stay just one year. Before they knew it, they had been in Bayonne five years and given 1,100 concerts throughout the United States. This portrait shows the Till brothers, Daniel and William, posing with their sisters, Annie and Miss Till, in front of the rockophones. The brothers began building the instruments around 1870, after their father, a stone-cutter, noticed that when he struck the rocks on Mount Skiddaw in England's Lake District, they produced musical tones. He and his sons began traveling to the mountain from their home in Derwentwater to collect rocks. Once they brought them home, they tuned them by chipping the ends of them to raise their tones, and cutting pieces from the middle of them to deepen them. By placing the tuned rocks on straw ropes attached to wooden stands, they created the rockaphone. Between 1875 and 1885, the Tills became known throughout Europe for their "rock music." After attending one of their 150 concerts at London's Crystal Palace, John Ruskin, the noted art critic, wrote the Tills to congratulate them: "you have given me a new insight into crystalline rock substances, also a new musical pleasure." In 1890, the band broke up when William and his wife decided to stay in Bayonne to raise their children (see p. 49), instead of returning to England with Daniel and the Miss Tills. Their farewell concert at the First Reformed Church included "Popular Airs" on the rockaphones, as well as other works on the chimes, the zither, and the musical glasses. The evening ended with a demonstration of Thomas Edison's new phonograph. William stayed in Bayonne for nearly thirty-five years, and in 1899 he formed a second rock band with his daughters (see p. 84). (Bayonne Public Library)

Herman and Sarah Klein, *c*. 1885. Herman poses seriously for this engagement portrait with the tall bowler hat and high-buttoned waistcoat that dominated men's fashion throughout the 1880s. Sarah is also fashionably dressed in a jacket and skirt with bead and braid trim. When he sat for this portrait, Herman was already a wealthy man, having opened the second travel agency in the United States at 220 E. 22nd Street (see p. 158). He helped many Hungarians enter the United States by sending them tickets with his agency's name and address that they could show the immigration authorities as proof that they had friends and jobs in America (see p. 121). Besides raising his family and managing his business, Herman also served as a justice of the peace and a health commissioner.

The Free Public Library of Bayonne, 1895. Twenty years after St. John's Church opened Bayonne's first private library on Broadway, the City decided to open a public library in the old city hall (see opposite), located at Broadway and 22nd Street. The first librarian, Alfred C. Herzog, oversaw a reading room and a 4,000 volume collection. In 1895, the City added books from Solon Humphreys' private library for workingmen on the Hook who wished to improve themselves. The library moved to its current site on Avenue C and 31st Street in 1904 (see p. 77). (Bayonne Public Library)

Hyman Lazarus (1870–1924), 1896. Hyman posed for this portrait when he became the chief of the Bayonne Fire Department, the youngest man ever to fill the post. Within a year of coming to Bayonne with his parents in 1880, Hyman began working after school as a barrel-roller on the Hook to help the family meet its expenses. Once he graduated from School No. 2 in 1884, he opened a cigar-making business on 21st Street and attended law school at night. Despite work and school, he still found time to organize the Centreville Athletic Club and serve as its president for four years. After he graduated from law school in 1894, he became a justice of the peace, then clerk to the recorder (or judge), and finally recorder (see p. 78). In 1910, he became the publisher of *The Bayonne Times* (see p. 147). (Bayonne Public Library)

City hall, 1894. When the City government outgrew the first city hall (see opposite), it decided to build this new hall in what was previously a cornfield at Avenue E and 30th Street. Although residents initially objected to placing the hall in such an isolated spot so near the germs of the Story Hospital (see p. 55), the entire city celebrated the hall's opening with a parade on Columbus Day, 1892. Huge crowds gathered to watch over three thousand people march from 1st to 51st Street alongside floats from various industries. The celebration ended with a dedication ceremony that included Mrs. Ogden Crane singing "Columbia" and Mr. Pearsall reading *The Charge of the Light Brigade*. (Bayonne Public Library)

The Central Railroad Roundhouse in July 1890. The Central Railroad built this roundhouse east of Avenue E (see p. 20) to service its engines when it laid tracks through Bayonne in 1864. The Central decided to lay rail through Bayonne in 1854 in order to provide a rail link between Elizabeth and Jersey City. The state legislature finally granted them permission to do so in 1860, after insisting that the bridge over Newark Bay from Elizabeth to Bayonne swing open to allow ships up the bay. When the 1 1/2-mile-long bridge was completed in 1864, it was the longest "swing" bridge in the world, with a 216-foot-long "swing" manned twenty-four hours a day by bridge-tenders. Once the bridge was finished, the Central began bringing workers from Elizabeth over it to lay tracks through Bayonne. All along the way, buildings were either moved or torn down to make way for the tracks. For months, explosions and dust from the construction work plagued city residents. Finally, on July 29, 1864, the Clinton rattled through Bayonne with the first trainload of passengers. Bayonnites could now travel to Manhattan in just thirty minutes, and almost any industry could now settle on the Hook, because the Central's cars could bring raw materials to Bayonne from across the country. After the Central opened Port Johnston in 1865, Bayonne industries were assured of a steady, cheap supply of coal to power their stills and furnaces. At the time, Port Johnston was the largest coal port in the world, with a 2,650-foot wharf that the Central built with the dirt it had removed to lay the tracks through Bayonne. (Newark Public Library)

A coal combine, c. 1894. This view of the Central Railroad's tracks from the Avenue A bridge looking east (see p. 117) shows hundreds of cars full of coal "combined," or linked together, waiting to be unloaded onto ships at Port Johnston (see opposite). Until it burned in July 1898, the wooden bridge over the tracks at Avenue A was such a popular meeting place for young couples that Bayonnites called it the "Lover's Bridge." (Bayonne Public Library)

The 8th Street station, c. 1890. After the Central built this station in the 1870s, trains for Elizabeth and New York stopped here every half hour from 6 am until midnight. Trains were occasionally delayed, as when a cow on the tracks held up a train for fifteen minutes in May, 1887. Bayonne still had enough farms for A.A. Smith to find it profitable to advertise his "Animal Feed, Hay, and Straw" on the billboard to the left. (Bayonne Public Library)

Orford Copper Company officials, 1890. When a copper strike in Canada interrupted their business in 1881, the Orford Copper Company opened this refinery on the Hook. The Company officials standing here are, from left to right: (front) T. Fudge and A. Gibb; (back) J. McNicoll, J. Patterson, C. Bartlett, D. Davis, Kane, J.L. Thompson, G. Smythe, F. Fletcher, and E. Fletcher. (Bayonne Historical Society)

The Orford Refining Furnace, 1890. Standing among the company officials at the center of this scene is Colonel R.M. Thomson, who oversaw the development of the "Orford Process" for separating nickel from copper. In 1880, the Colonel began looking for such a process for the United States government, which needed nickel for the refrigeration machinery it was using on a hospital ship during a yellow fever epidemic in New Orleans. By 1910, Bayonne led the country in the production of nickel and nickel alloys. (Bayonne Historical Society)

The Orford Refining Furnace, 1890. W. David stands on the left overseeing the Orford workers pumping air into the furnace. After trains brought raw copper ore to the Hook from mines in Pima, Arizona, the men heated the ore in the furnace until it melted into a thick liquid. They then refined it by skimming the impurities off the top of it. (Bayonne Historical Society)

The Orford Cupola Furnace, 1890. T. Saunders (foreman) on the left and G. O'Neil (furnaceman) pose next to the Orford Cupola Furnace, remelting metals before casting. In 1898, Captain Edward E. Van Buskirk petitioned the company to install new chimneys in the furnaces, arguing that the sulfuric acid gases they emitted were destroying his family's farm (see p. 22). Edward told *The Bayonne Herald* "where I used to gather forty or fifty crates" of tomatoes a day, "now I don't pick eight." (Bayonne Historical Society)

Standard Oil workers, *c.* 1895. Whereas the Irish immigrants of the 1860s found work with the railroad (see p. 29), the Hungarian, Czech, and Slovak immigrants of the 1880s found work with companies such as Standard (see p. 31), Tidewater, and Ocean Oil on the Hook. Most of these jobs were dangerous; the newspapers of the day were filled with reports of workers being burned by exploding stills or crushed by heavy machinery. These immigrants pose in their hats, suits, and ties outside one of Standard's buildings. Like all the eastern European immigrants working on the Hook, they would have been known generally as "Bohemians," regardless of their nationality. An 1881 *Bayonne Herald* story noted that since so many of them could not speak English and their names were so difficult to pronounce, their employers referred to them by numbers. The same *Herald* story described a group of seventy-five "Bohemians" who "form[ed] a sort of colony by themselves," sleeping in one room, doing their own cooking, and "keep[ing] as much to themselves as they are permitted to do." Like immigrants before and after them, the "Bohemians" found that living cheaply with their fellow immigrants let them save money from their small salaries—most made less than a $1 a day in 1895—to pay for their families to come to America (see p. 121). Living in "colonies" also helped them adjust to the new language and customs of America together. Between 1860 and 1900, as Irish and Germans, then "Bohemians," and later Poles, Russians, and Ukranians came to Bayonne, these colonies of immigrants sprung up on the Hook from Avenues F to I along E. 22nd Street (see p. 115). Italian immigrants, who arrived largely between 1885 and 1910 (see p. 85), found work in construction and settled along 23rd and 50th Streets. (Bayonne Public Library)

The E. 49th Street train station, *c.* 1895. Many immigrants to Bayonne entered the city through this train station at E. 49th Street. Before the Ellis Island Immigration Center opened in 1892, immigrants reached Bayonne by either ferry or train after landing at Castle Garden, an island off Manhattan. Once Ellis Island opened, immigrants could just cross a footbridge to reach Jersey City and board a train for the seven minute ride to Bayonne. (Bayonne Public Library)

Rosalia Zurumski Oleskie, *c.* 1895. Rosalia, who emigrated from Poznan, Poland, looks charming in this silk dress with puffed sleeves and braid trim. She may have had this portrait taken for her wedding to Wladyslaw Oleskie (b. 1872), who had come to Bayonne with his father, Michael, in the 1870s (see p. 30). The Oleskies raised their three children in Bayonne, where Wladyslaw worked as the foreman for Bixby and Marshall (see p. 129). (Bill James)

49

The Bayonne Cyclones, 1894. Among these twelve members of the Cyclone's undefeated 1894 football team sit E. Allen, A. Webb, and Walter Till (see p. 41). Walter helped the Cyclones beat the Orange Eleven in November 1894 by scoring three touchdowns and four field goals. Like most football teams at the time, the team wore just boots, padded trousers, and jerseys (see p. 68). (Bayonne Public Library)

The Newark Bay Boat Club, c. 1893. This horse and carriage stands on the southeastern side of the boat club's house on Newark Bay at W. 24th Street. Like the New Jersey Yacht Club, the Newark Club was drawn to Bayonne because of its reputation as a yachting center. When the club built this house in 1890, it designed the veranda on the left so that club members could sit on it and watch boats on the bay from 8th Street to Jersey City. On the waterfront below the veranda, they built docks, a boat basin, and a marine railroad. Every night, the caretaker of the club lit four red glass windows in a tower on the northwest corner of the house to greet the club's members across the bay. (Bayonne Public Library)

Going fishing, c. 1898. The Vreelands and their friends pose in the yard of their home at 74 W. 32nd Street before a fishing expedition on Newark Bay, which lies in the background. With their nets, buckets, and poles, they seem ready for anything—Frank even holds a gun. Vreelands have been fishing on Newark Bay at least since 1812, when Henry Vreeland built a home on 25th Street (see p. 122). They may have begun even earlier, for Michael was a descendent of Michael Jansen Vreeland, who left Holland for America in 1646. (C.L. Vreeland)

Cleaning fish, c. 1898. The Vreelands take a break from cleaning eels to pose for this picture in front of the corn in their garden. Michael, ever the gentleman in his shirt and tie (center), waits for the picture before cleaning the eel in his left hand, whereas the unidentified man on the left plunges right in. The plants hanging from the post behind Billy and Frank (right) were probably herbs hung to dry. (C.L. Vreeland)

School No. 6 in June 1895. These students celebrated the end of school with a pageant in which Lottie Muchler sang "That Jone's Boy" and W.E. Muchler sang "When I'm a Man." The students posed here at the school with their teacher Miss Jessie Wheeler (right). The graduates were Isabelle Braunstein, Alte Collins, Mattie Farless, Robert Gay, John Kiddie, F.L. Melville, Fred Noonan, Martha Ohning, Robert Schlereth, Catherine R. Stewart, Clarence Van Deusen, and Fannie Warden. The testimonial recipients were Seth Anderson, George Comfort, Pauline Flugel, Florence Marsel, Robert Meier, Lottie Mutchler, Nora Ryan, Laura See, Louise Selling, William Varian, Alma Weldig, Emma White, and Lottie Wilson. (Bayonne Public Library)

The Trinity Episcopal Church, c. 1893. After a fire destroyed the first Trinity Church in 1879, the congregation built this new brown stone Gothic building. The first service in this church was the wedding of Solon Humphreys' son Edward (b. 1848) to Mary Duane on June 8, 1881. The ceremony began as Edward, in a "Prince Albert" suit, watched Mary walk down the aisle to "Lohengrin" march. (Bayonne Public Library)

The Bose drugstore, *c.* 1895. Anna and Charles Bose stand in front of their store at the corner of Broadway and 21st Street. One of Charles' first jobs as a pharmacist was at a branch of W.C. Alper's drugstore on the Hook (see p. 40). When he opened his own store, Charles developed the "Bose Emulsion" advertised in the window on the left for 25 or 50¢. He used the two-headed goat on the pressed-back chair (center) to attract customers to the store. (Bayonne Public Library)

Anna and Charles Bose, *c.* 1895. This detail from the picture above reveals a cat sitting in the store just behind Charles' left knee. Anna's suit shows how fashion shifted in the 1890s as the new "hourglass figure" replaced the bustle as the ideal silhouette. This new style emphasized women's corseted waistlines by enlarging the tops of the sleeves and the bottoms of the skirts on their dresses. (Bayonne Public Library)

Solon (1821–1900) and Mary Ellen Walsh (d. 1915) Humphreys, c. 1896. The Humphreys pose on the estate that they built in 1856 on Newark Bay between 10th and 11th Street after Solon accepted a post with the Wall Street firm of New York Governor E.D. Morgan. They had married in 1846 in Mary's hometown, St. Louis, where Solon had settled to work with the railroads. Besides designing the trunk line system and promoting the Ohio and Missouri Railroads, he also served as an officer in several railroad companies. (Bayonne Public Library)

Pepperidge, c. 1896. These two men enjoy the view of Newark Bay from the porch of Pepperidge, named after the pepper trees that filled the site. The Humphreys opened Pepperidge several times a year so that organizations such as Story Hospital could hold benefits on its grounds. In 1895, Trinity Church held an international festival here, with music and dances from countries around the world. Another benefit featured dancing around a May pole in the yard. (Bayonne Public Library)

Story Hospital, c. 1898. Before this hospital opened on 30th Street (see p. 27), residents had to travel by horse to Jersey City or by boat to Bellevue Hospital, New York, for treatment. The hospital's first patient, Mrs. Wenzerberger of 19th Street, arrived on the night of March 10, 1890. She had fallen on W. 20th Street, which *The Bayonne Herald* described as a "dismal, dangerous road by night." Dr. Luce set her leg with splints that he made from wooden boxes—the hospital was still waiting for its supplies to arrive. (A. Resnick)

Dr. Lucius Donohoe (1868–1951), c. 1898. Although Lucius enjoys a leisurely drive here, he was usually so anxious to reach his patients that he trained his horses to start trotting as soon as his left foot hit the floorboard. Before he bought a car in 1904, Lucius broke several bones in accidents while tearing through Bayonne in this calash (or carriage) while making house calls. (Bayonne Public Library)

The Morris Canal, c. 1898. This view of a mule boat tied beneath the Boulevard Bridge over the canal looks west toward Newark; the towpath on the left ran along the Bayonne shore of the canal. The canal had a weak current, so the boats needed mules to pull them along. The man holding the mule on the towpath was the mule "driver," who led the mules at 3 to 4-miles per hour as they pulled the boat behind them. The man at the front of the boat was probably the captain, who stayed in the boat working the tiller (or steering lever) to keep the boat from ramming into the banks. Most captains owned their boats and lived in 6-by-9-foot cabins at the back of them (like this one) with their families (see p. 33). Mule boats began traveling past Bayonne in 1836, when the Morris Canal Company opened an 8-mile extension of the canal from Newark to Jersey City. Canal workers, mostly Irish immigrants, spent two years digging the 40-foot wide, 5-foot deep canal bed by hand, using nothing more than picks and shovels. When the extension past Bayonne was finished, the 106.69-mile-long canal between Phillipsburg and Jersey City became New Jersey's longest manmade waterway. For the next thirty years, the canal was packed with barges hauling iron, coal, and agricultural supplies across northern New Jersey. As the railroad began shipping goods in the 1860s, however, canal traffic began to decline (see p. 44). A train could travel across the state in just five hours, whereas a canal barge took five days. Between 1860 and 1875, the amount of freight shipped on the canal dropped from 606,631 to 461,816 tons. The last mule boat passed through Bayonne in 1907, and the State finally drained the canal in 1924. (Jersey City Library)

A stroll along the canal, *c.* 1898. With the Avenue C bridge in the distance, these young ladies sit along the Bayonne bank of the canal enjoying the shade on a warm summer afternoon. Well into the twentieth century, Bayonnites escaped the heat by sleeping in tents along the canal. In the winter, skating parties took over the scene. (Bayonne Public Library)

The canal bridge, *c.* 1890. William Armbruster took this photograph of men posing on the Avenue C bridge over the canal. In the background lie the fields and hedgerows of the Vreeland farm in Bayonne, which served as a movie set for Centaur films (see p. 94) before being divided into 49th and 50th Streets. (Bayonne Public Library)

Left: Honorah Crimmins, c. 1895.
Right: Strauch harness store, c. 1897.
After he wed Honorah Crimmins (left), an emigrant from Limerick, Ireland, John Strauch opened this harness shop at 242 Broadway in 1897. John, an emigrant from Berlin, Germany, made harnesses and saddles to sell in the store, as well as all but one set of harness for the Bayonne Fire Department. As automobiles began to replace horses between 1910 and 1920 (see p. 92), John's son Joseph shifted the business from harnesses to luggage and book-bags. (M. McGlynn)

Digging out on February 14, 1899. With his handlebar moustache frozen into place, James Davenport (b. 1844) shovels the walk of School No. 3. This view looking east on 49th Street shows the aftermath of a snowstorm that began on Sunday, February 12, and continued until the morning of Tuesday, February 14. The snow fell so heavily that ten Staten Islanders spent Monday night stuck in the ferry house after the trains, ferries, and trollies closed (see p. 25). The children on the left returned to school on Wednesday morning. (Bayonne Public Library)

Goldenhorn Brothers in December 1899. In the nineteenth century, most shops simply arranged their merchandise in a pretty pattern for Christmas. Samuel Goldenhorn and his wife Emma used lace doilies as a backdrop for this display of frames, boxes, collars, and cuffs. Before electric washing machines were available, people reduced the amount of laundry they did by hand by wearing shirts with detachable collars and cuffs, which they could change daily. (Bayonne Public Library)

School No. 5, c. 1899. After decorating their blackboard with garlands, this class gathered at the table with their slates and books for this Christmas picture. Some of the students who attended this school on the Hook in 1899 were Louis Heitman, Maggie Rigney, Rudolph Kukla, Mary Wagner, Harvey Miller, Ernestine Cohn, and Samuel Klein. (Bayonne Public Library)

The Ideal Billiard Parlor, *c.* 1899. The owner of this pool hall, David Horsley (1873–1933), stands at the right in the doorway. In 1907, he opened the first independent movie studio in the country here at 900 Broadway (see p. 94). The young man standing on the far left is probably David's brother Harry (b. 1881), who began living with David in 1898. The Horsleys emigrated with their parents from England in 1884, after David lost part of his left arm in a train accident. Once in Bayonne, David's father began working as a timekeeper at Tidewater Oil, and David became a paper-boy. After his father's death, David's mother married John H. Shipley, a ship caulker, and opened a variety store at 1013 Broadway. (Bison Archives)

The Bergen Point ferry, 1899. This crowd has probably assembled on 1st Street to see the new ferryboat docked in the background, the *B.M. Shanley*, which began running between Bayonne and Port Richmond on June 10, 1899. Behind the carriage and livery van on the right stands one of the electric trolley cars that began driving on Avenue C between 1st Street and Jersey City in 1894. Before the electric cars began running, horse cars made the trip. (Bayonne Public Library)

Three
The City in the
New Century
1900–1909

The Firemen's parade, May 15, 1901. When the Exempt Firemen of New Jersey held their annual convention in Bayonne in 1901, the City decided to hold this parade. To welcome their guests from around the state, Bayonnites began decorating their homes with streamers and bunting a full week before the parade began. These bystanders watch Bayonne's Protection Engine Company No. 5 march up Broadway near 5th Street as a band plays in the wagon behind them (see p. 66). (Bayonne Public Library)

School No. 2, *c*. 1900. This class poses seriously with their books at their wrought-iron desks. The girl in the starched pinafore on the right in the front row is Anna E. Bose (see p. 53). Some of the other students are Jacob Miller, Celia Rade, August Ruhlmann, and Albert Wauters. To see what the students were doing at all times, their teacher, Miss A.A. Freure, sits to the side of the class as teaching manuals of the day recommended. (Bayonne Public Library)

The Bethlehem Mission Juniors, *c*. 1900. These junior members stand with their banner and the American flag on the steps of the Bethlehem Mission at Avenue C near 26th Street, the boys in their caps and girls in their wide-brimmed hats. Mrs. Gilberta A. Dallas (d. 1908) started the mission in her home on 27th Street around 1880. After Charles Winfield donated land for this building in 1883, Bayonne's Dutch Reformed churches used it for Sunday school classes, prayer meetings, and charity work. (Bayonne Public Library)

Left: Herman Klein, *c.* 1902.
Right: Frances Klein, *c.* 1902.
As befits one of Bayonne's most successful businessmen, Herman wears a stylish black frock coat with grey striped trousers and a silk top hat for this portrait (see p. 42). On the right, his youngest daughter, Frances, peers shyly at the camera from beneath her tall bonnet.

The Enterprise Hose Company, *c.* 1900. With neighborhood children clowning behind them, these Enterprise volunteers pose in front of their firehouse at 22nd Street near Avenue I (see p. 20). Along with the Washington Engine Company a few blocks west, "Enterprise" battled all the industrial fires on the Hook (see p. 64). No matter where they were, the firemen dropped everything to rush to the firehouse when the fire bell rang. One dedicated volunteer even leapt out of a dentist's chair without waiting for his fillings to fight a fire. (Bayonne Fire Museum)

The Standard Oil fire of July 5, 1900. The boy on the left watches as smoke pours from the oil tanks behind the Van Buskirk home (see p. 22) during the great Standard Oil fire, which began around midnight on Wednesday, July 4, 1900. After suffering through one of the hottest Fourth of Julys ever recorded, Bayonnites must have cheered when rain began to fall around midnight. The day had been a sweltering 95 degrees, and the high humidity had only increased after a storm passed in the afternoon. During the afternoon storm, one bolt of lightning had struck the Statue of Liberty, while another had set the Brady Brother's storehouse on Staten Island ablaze. The lightning that hit Bayonne during the midnight storm, however, threatened to destroy the entire Hook: when it struck, it created a fireball that crashed through the front of Lizzie Cumming's saloon, the Bay View House, at 435 E. 22nd Street. The fireball flew through the Bay View, out the back wall, and ricochetted from the ground to strike three Standard Oil tanks near 22nd Street. Within seconds, burning oil from the 40,000-gallon tanks spread across the yard to send seven other tanks exploding into flames. As she fled the Bay View with her two children, Lizzie Cummings scalded her feet on the flaming oil. When Bayonne's firemen arrived minutes later, the heat from the 200-foot-high flames was so intense that it blistered the paint on the wheels of their fire trucks. Just a block away lay the Hook Village (see p. 48), where over 4,500 people lived along 22nd Street between Center Street and Avenue I (see p. 115). The force of the explosions shattered windows throughout the village, driving the terrified residents into the street in their nightclothes. As a New York Times reporter noted, living in the village was like living "on the edge of a volcano." By dawn, the villagers began fleeing to the meadows northeast of the village for safety; this photograph shows people sitting with their furniture in front of the Van Buskirk home. By Thursday afternoon, the only person the Times reporter could find in the village was a German grocer sleeping in his doorway. When the reporter asked the grocer if he was afraid, he said, "Vat's der use? If it goes oop, it goes oop. I can't help it." (Bayonne Public Library)

The Standard Oil fire. As the temperature climbed into the 90s on Thursday, flaming oil continued to spread the fire throughout Standard's yard. Around dawn, a new danger arose when a westerly breeze began carrying the fire away from the village towards New York Bay. Once the flaming oil reached the shore, it moved quickly across the top of the water, burning everything in its path. If enough oil poured into the water, the entire harbor could burst into flames. At one point during the afternoon, a strip of flame-topped water stretched a mile from the Hook toward the Statue of Liberty. Standing on the shore, Wal Van Buskirk watched in horror as another strip rushed toward the mouth of the Kill where his brother Phil lay sleeping aboard his sloop. Without wasting a minute, Wal grabbed a rowboat and headed toward the sloop. He reached it just in time to climb on board, hoist the anchor, and sail out of danger. By late Thursday afternoon the crisis in the bay had passed after Standard employees dropped log booms in a semi-circle around the shore to contain the overflowing oil. Meanwhile, other employees began digging 10-foot-wide and 6-foot-deep trenches through Standard's yard (as the men do here) to contain the oil overflowing from the tanks. When the trenches were finished, the men emptied the oil into them by shooting cannon balls into the tanks. The trenches then carried the oil to container basins in the meadows where it could burn itself out safely. By Thursday evening, the fire began to draw sightseers from around the region. Crowds gathered all along the shores of the bay to watch the flames. Others rode back and forth across the bay on ferryboats. One man on the roof garden of Koster and Bial's in lower Manhattan claimed that he could read his newspaper by the light of the flames on the Hook. By Friday evening, the fire finally stopped spreading, and by ten o'clock Saturday evening, the fire ended. Despite the explosions, the flaming oil, and the smoke, only twenty-two people were hurt during the seventy-hour blaze. (Bayonne Public Library)

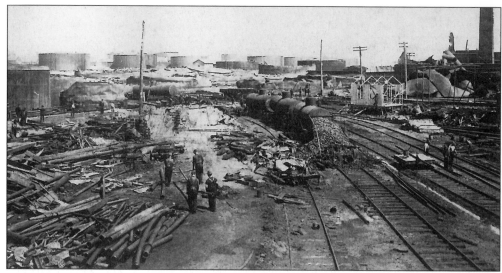

The Standard Oil fire on July 8, 1900. Besides losing twenty-five tanks, a boiler shop, and a paraffine building, Standard also lost several tons of coal and dozens of railroad cars in the fire. As the executives on the left inspect the $2.5 million in damages at the refinery, the workmen in the foreground begin cleaning up charred railroad siding. This view of the yard looks northwest towards E. 22nd Street; the rooftops of the Hook Village appear faintly behind the tanks in the background. (Bayonne Public Library)

The Firemen's parade, May 15, 1901. Several boys tag behind these volunteers from Bayonne's Independence Engine Company as they pull their first steam pumper over the trolley tracks on Broadway (see p. 61). So that everyone could watch the parade, Bayonne's schools, offices, and industries closed for the day. (Bayonne Public Library)

Company I, 4th Regiment, July 18, 1901. The forty-nine men of Bayonne's regiment of the New Jersey National Guard stand in formation in front of their headquarters at 505 Broadway, the old Oliver Homestead. By 9:00 am, they began marching to Sea Girt under Captain James R. Gatchel (left) for a regimental encampment at Camp Voorhees. They carried their clothes, plates, and silverware in the haversacks draped over their shoulders. (Bayonne Fire Museum)

Street repairs, 1900. As a trolley wends up the block, these men prepare to lay curbing on 5th Street. At the turn of the century, some of Bayonne's streets had Belgian block pavement (see p. 63), but most were still dirt roads. After these men put the curbing in place, they "macadamized" the road by spreading the piles of stone in back of them over it. In 1902, Avenue C became the first asphalted road in Bayonne. (Bayonne Public Library)

The Bergen Point Field Club, c. 1901. Like other football teams at the time, the Pointers' uniform consisted simply of shirts, padded trousers, and boots, though one of these players does have a nose guard. Football was truly a dangerous sport in the days before helmets or shoulder pads. In 1902, two Bayonne teenagers, Harry Devine and William Albrect, died as the result of football injuries. (Bayonne Public Library)

The Bergen Point Lighthouse, c. 1905. When the United States opened this 54-foot tower in 1850, the President appointed Peter Girth as the first keeper (see p. 20). Like the twelve keepers who followed him (see p. 35), Peter lived with his family in a six-room house attached to the light. Every evening at sunset, he lit two kerosene lamps at the top of the light to help boats navigate the treacherous currents around the rock ledges in the Kill. Robert Gray (b. 1874) vanished in the currents while rowing ashore for groceries just two weeks after he became the keeper in February 1902. His aunt and children, stranded on the light without food, had to signal for help by raising the American flag upside down. After the last keeper, Hans Beuthe, retired in 1941, the United States demolished the light as part of its project to blast and dredge the Kill. (Bayonne Public Library)

Philip Elsworth, *c.* 1900. Philip (left) and his friend seem to enjoy relaxing with their pipes on this stoop. Philip grew up in his parents Philip and Lydia's home on New York Bay at 36th Street (see p. 37). After graduating from high school in 1890, he began working for Standard Oil rather than his father's oyster business (see p. 36). Around 1900, Philip was killed in a tank explosion at Standard. (Bayonne Public Library)

A grocery store, *c.* 1900. Although these children seem to enjoy posing outside this family grocery, the man on the left looks anxious to get back to business. By 1903, Bayonne had over 173 of these small stores scattered throughout the city. This one advertises "White Rose Tea" beneath the signs for fruit, oysters, and clams in the windows. The signs flanking the door advertise ammonia and naphtha, while the box on the left announces "p-e-a-s." (Bayonne Public Library)

A political cartoon from October 1903. Democratic mayoral candidate Thomas Brady stands impassively, ignoring the attacks of the Fusionist gremlins opposing him in this cartoon by Charles L. Kling of 34th Street. The *Bayonne Herald* ran this cartoon several times during the election. As it suggests, the *Herald*'s coverage was anything but impartial. On the front page, it urged its readers to "Be men, not monkeys—vote for Brady." It even ran Brady songs, such as this verse sung to the tune of the "Battle Hymn of the Republic": "Yes, we're gladly fighting for the glory of Bayonne. And voting for a party that the railroad does not own. And a man who'll give his service to-o-o the town alone, We vote for honest Tom." The *Herald*'s rival, the *Bayonne Times*, was equally biased in its support of the Fusionist candidate, Pierre P. Garven. After the *Herald* accused Garven, an attorney for Central Railroad, of being a stooge for industry, the *Times* accused Brady of creating the dangerous coal shortage of 1902 to help his family's coal business. Once Brady won the election by four hundred votes, the *Herald* reported how the Fusionists would satisfy their campaign bets: Steve Harcobus had to kiss a mule; Harry Mayes had to give Neil O'Donnell his Sunday coat and hat; Dick Warren had to sweep two blocks of Broadway for Harry Mainhard; and lawyer James F. McCabe had to stand on one foot bleating like a goat for fifteen minutes on Broadway. In 1905 Garven ran again and became the youngest mayor in Bayonne history. He served as mayor until 1909, then again from 1915 to 1919. (Bayonne Public Library)

Left: Sergeant Martin J. Cassidy (1864–1926), c. 1903.
Right: Captain Michael F. Reilly (1861–1921), c. 1903.
Ten years after he joined the force, Martin was promoted to sergeant on December 1, 1903, the day Michael was promoted from sergeant to captain. Michael had moved to Bayonne in 1874. He worked as a plumber and a tinsmith, then became a policeman in 1888. After he became the chief of the force in 1914, he gained national attention for holding off a mob of five hundred people during the Standard Oil Strike of 1916 (see p. 125). (Bayonne Police Department)

Left: Patrolman Edward J. Wirth, c. 1903.
Right: Patrolman Richard E. Lee, 1903.
Edward and Richard became patrolmen in 1893 when the uniform still included these "Bobby" hats, and patrolmen still enforced the 12-mile-per-hour speed limit for bicycles, horses, and automobiles. By 1903, they were not only nabbing the cherry thieves who pilfered Trask's orchard at 75 Broadway, but also levying fines on boys who used pea-shooters—outlawed in 1896—and girls under sixteen who attended dance halls without guardians. (Bayonne Police Department)

A c. 1904 photograph of a basketball team. These muscular players could be the members of the "Cadets of Temperance" team, which posed for photographer Frank Davis in October 1904. The Cadets played at the West Side Athletic Club courts on W. 11 Street, along with other teams like the "Hummers." Hundreds of spectators attended the games, which were usually followed by parties and dances. (Bayonne Public Library)

Joyriding, c. 1900. These children seem to be enjoying their drive as they pause at the Boulevard near 6th Street. Dr. Walter F. Robinson identified the animal with the flags in its ears pulling their cart as "Woodward's Goat." (Bayonne Public Library)

Bayonne Hook and Ladder Company No. 1, c. 1905. Bob Milden mans the "tiller" and Bill Smeaton holds the horses as this truck pulls out of the firehouse onto W. 47th Street. No. 1 received this 55-foot extension ladder truck in October 1905. The truck was so long, it needed a "tiller," or rear steering wheel, to turn corners. Standing on the sideboard are, from left to right, John Cubberly, George Morecraft, Vedder Van Dyke, Jr., Sam O'Dell, and J. Edward Woodruff. (Bayonne Fire Museum)

An organ grinder, c. 1900. This young gentleman and a dog enjoy the organ music the man in the center plays. Organ grinders roamed the streets of Bayonne well into this century. (Bayonne Public Library)

The Heraty family, c. 1903. While his father sits in the rocker, Joseph H. Heraty (left) poses with his wife, Clara, and their daughters Edna and Mabel on the porch of their home at 930 Avenue C. Like many people, the Heratys moved uptown after industries such as Babcox and Wilcox settled at the Point around 1900. As Joseph explained to the *Bayonne Herald* when he moved here in 1902, the Point had become the "business end of town." (Bayonne Historical Society)

Broadway, c. 1905. Around the turn of the century, a new business district began to emerge here, at 33rd Street (see above). This view looks north on Broadway, with delivery wagons parked outside Perry's Ice Cream Shop (on the left) and Drake's Business College (on the right). Across 33rd Street from Drake's stands the Bayonne Bank, built in 1904. Further up Broadway on the right, A.D. Woodruff's advertises "Prudential Life Insurance" on the side of its building. At the time, Woodruff's sold roast beef for 18¢ a pound. (Bayonne Public Library)

Left: Eugene Daniel Harding, c. 1900. Because his father died before he was born (see p. 30), Eugene and his mother lived with his grandfather, J.H. Brower, over his store on 33rd Street near Broadway. (J. O'Donnell)

Right: The Ryan family, c. 1905. Mrs. Ryan poses with the oldest and youngest of her eight children, Mary Ryan McGlynn and Joseph. (M. McGlynn)

C.G. Hendrickson's, c. 1905. Charles Hendrickson stands outside his saloon with his children, Clarence and Florence, looking towards the corner of Broadway and 31st Street (see p. 33). The man in the apron on the right was probably a bartender in the saloon. The sign over the door advertises C. Trefz Fine Lager beer, while the sign on the telephone pole advertises the pay phone that Charles installed in the saloon in 1904. (R. Capriola)

Augustus K. and Ina D. Barstow, c. 1903. The Barstows pose among the daisies and sweet peas in the garden of their home at 816 Broadway near 37th Street. The son of Wisconsin Governor William A. Barstow, Augustus came to Bayonne in 1881 when he succeeded his father-in-law, Charles Stillman, as the superintendent of the paraffine department at Standard Oil. Augustus worked for Standard until he died of pneumonia in 1906 at the age of fifty-seven. (Bayonne Public Library)

The Barstow home, c. 1903. The floral wallpaper, Axminster carpets, and fringed curtains in the Barstow's sitting rooms show how a well-to-do home looked at the turn of the century. The Barstow's son Joseph probably spent many happy evenings in the Bentwood child's rocker in front of the marble fireplace. The glass front piece in the room on the left was a music box. (Bayonne Public Library)

Carnegie Library, c. 1904. As Bayonne's population leapt from 19,033 in 1890 to 32,722 in 1900, the library in the old city hall became crowded (see p. 42). After receiving a generous donation from industrialist Andrew Carnegie, Bayonne built this new library at Avenue C and 31st Street. The library played a critical role in helping Bayonne's immigrants learn English. In 1905, Bayonne's illiteracy rate was four times the national average: forty percent of the residents could neither read nor write. (Resnick)

The Robinson home, 1905. Mrs. Robinson sits in a rocker on the porch of her home at 93 E. 44th Street, where Bayonne historian Walter F. Robinson was born. Her husband, Arthur H., was one of fifteen farmers in Bayonne in 1905 (see p. 143). (L. Fahley)

Recorder's court, November 5, 1905. These men pose in the courtroom at the new police headquarters at Avenue C and 26th Street. Frank Davis (see p. 93) took this photograph after the first case was dismissed for a lack of evidence by Hyman Lazarus, the recorder (or judge), who sits behind the bench at the center of this photograph. Over the years, Hyman developed quite a reputation on the bench (see p. 143). When a tenement fire broke out on Avenue C between 18th and 19th Streets in December 1903, Hyman not only recessed court so that he and the other men could help fight the blaze, but also helped the forty families left homeless by the fire find lodging at the Hebrew Institute nearby (see p. 43). The next day, he brought them clothing and a roast beef dinner. Hyman usually tried to let defendants tell their own story in their own way. Since he spoke several languages, he rarely needed an interpreter, and he even used sign language with deaf defendants. Once Hyman decided a defendant was guilty, though, he was determined to apply a fit punishment, whatever that may be. During one trial he asked the defendant, an accused wife beater, to follow him back to his chambers (behind the door on the right in this photograph). After Hyman closed the door, everyone in the courtroom began to hear furniture crashing. When the men returned to the courtroom a few minutes later, Hyman was rolling down his sleeve, and the defendant had a black eye. The officials in this photograph are, from left to right: (standing around Hyman in the back row) Captain Michael Reilly (see p. 71), Court Officer Charles Melando, and Captain McBride; (standing in the front row) three unidentified men, City Attorney Noonan, Detective Patrick Gallagher, Detective E. M. Griffin, and Chief of Police Thomas Magner; (seated at the desk to the right) Recorder's Clerk Hugh Mara, who later became a city commissioner. (Bayonne Public Library)

Hyman Lazarus, November 21, 1905. Hyman addressed this picture to a fan club for Theodore Roosevelt, the "Little Roosevelt Club . . . Consisting of Marion Ripps, 13 yr; Anna Luther, 13 year; and Eva Feinburg, 14 years." Upon becoming president after the assassination of William McKinley in 1901, Theodore Roosevelt became so popular with children throughout the country that they began buying stuffed "Teddy" bears by the thousands. In Bayonne, the Bethlehem Mission Juniors held a series of "Roosevelt Rally Days" to support their hero (see p. 62). (Bayonne Public Library)

Alfred Young, 1906. Alfred holds the reins for this hose-wagon in front of Engine Company No. 3 at Broadway and 27th Street. When Bayonne established a full-time, paid fire department in September 1906, Alfred became a driver for $720 a year. Like the other members of the new force, he worked twenty-three hours a day and slept on the second floor of the firehouse. He received one day off a week and a ten-day vacation each year. (Bayonne Fire Department)

The Newark Bay shore, c. 1905. Swimmers used the bathing houses beneath the boat house in the background to change into their bathing costumes. One afternoon in 1903, two men caught over five hundred crabs off this shore at W. 28th Street. In 1923, the City began building the junior high school here. (A. Resnick)

Standard Oil, *c.* 1905. After the 1900 fire, Standard quickly rebuilt its plant on the Hook, so that by 1905 over 3,000 employees were refining 44,000 barrels of oil a day here. Standard's works helped make Bayonne the third largest manufacturing city in the New Jersey and the largest producer of refined oil in the country. (A. Resnick)

Tidewater workers, *c.* 1907. John Dittrich (second row from the back, fourth from the right) stands with his coworkers outside one of Tidewater Oil's buildings on the Hook. Like most of the industries on the Hook, Tidewater used boys for a variety of jobs. The United States did not prohibit children under sixteen from working in manufacturing plants until 1938. (P.G. Nowicki)

The New York Bay shore, c. 1907. These boys pull a rowboat through Odell's Cove along the shore about 43rd Street. This view of the shore originally formed the left half of a larger photograph; the right half is opposite. Part of the three-story building in the background, the Cadmus home, was built around 1730 and believed to have been a stop on the underground railroad. In 1902 the building became the clubhouse for the Pavonia Yacht Club (see p. 105). (Bayonne Public Library)

Fish's tower, c. 1907. Along with the photograph on the opposite page, this view of the New York Bay shore at E. 44th Street originally formed the left half of a larger photograph. The tall building on the right was Captain Robert Fish's tower house (see p. 36). Robert must have enjoyed his view of the bay as he sat each evening at the top of the tower. To the left of his boat house along the water is the Bayswater Hotel (see opposite) and then the Cadmus home (see above). (Bayonne Public Library)

The Bayswater, *c.* 1907. David Allen, the owner of the Bayswater Hotel (in the background), once served his customers a 36.5-pound lobster that he had caught off this dock at E. 44th Street. David Salter had originally built two sections of this building in the 1850s as homes for Captain William Elsworth. After Captain Robert Fish bought the property, he built a boat shop between the homes (see p. 36). In 1889, two English emigrants turned the site into a restaurant and hotel. (Bayonne Public Library).

Robbin's Reef Yacht Club, *c.* 1907. The flag waves in front of the Robbin's Reef clubhouse at the foot of E. 47th Street. The club was organized at the Bayswater Hotel in August 1906 and bought this house the following year. Every evening, club members gathered around this flagpole and watched the Robbin's Reef Lighthouse (see p. 18). When the light began flashing at sunset, the members set off a cannon and lowered the flag. (Bayonne Public Library)

The Till Family Rock Band, c. 1907. A few years after his brother and sisters returned to England (see p. 41), William Till started a second rock band with three of his four daughters. This promotional card for the band shows William with, left to right, Mildred, Esther, and Greta, posing in their lawn blouses with stand collars. Mildred sang contralto and Esther sang soprano. Greta, the youngest, began her career in 1901 when she starred with Irving Cadmus in a staging of Tom Thumb's wedding. The production also featured Anna Bose as Greta's bridesmaid (see p. 62) and Florence Hendrickson as her flower girl (see p. 75). (Bayonne Public Library)

The Westside Cadets, 1908. The team poses in their uniforms with their bat boy in the center. When the Cadets organized in 1902, they bought the Edgewater Golf Course and turned it into a baseball field for their games. Their new field on W. 10th Street between the Boulevard and Avenue C became known as "West Side Park." (Bayonne Public Library)

A 1908 photograph of Assumption 1st Communion. Reverend Michael T. Mercolino stands in the center of the back row, surrounded by the communicants and their families. Father Mercolino began celebrating Mass for Bayonne's Italian immigrants in June 1902 at a store at 92 W. 21st Street. He dedicated the first Assumption church in December 1903. (Bayonne Public Library)

School No. 7 in June 1908. Morris Brodman preserved this photograph of the graduates posing with their diplomas. Principal Samuel A. Roberson stands on the left. As Bayonne's population grew, so did the number of students in its schools: whereas seventeen students graduated from this school in 1901, thirty-one graduated in 1908. (Bayonne Public Library)

Melville Park, 1907. Frank Melville built this 150-foot-high gate on the Boulevard at 50th Street when he reopened Arlington Park as Melville Park in 1907. When lit, the 5,000 electric lights strung around the huge globe at the top of the gate could be seen as far away as Long Island. Since the park's 30,000 lights used more power than the rest of Bayonne, the Public Service Company built a plant just to light the park. The lights were just one of the features Frank added to the 16-acre park. By opening day (May 25th), he had spent $250,00 to add a flying swing, a carousel, a dancing pavilion, an old mill, and a theater for Thomas Alva Edison's new "moving pictures." The main attraction, though, was the scenic railway, the second largest in the country. The sign to the left of the gate advertises the opening of E.A. Schiller's new Opera House on Broadway at 23rd Street. (A. Resnick)

Another 1907 view of Melville Park. To the right of the buggy, waiters stand next to several men in straw boaters on the veranda of the Park Cafe. Many people enjoyed relaxing at the cafe after witnessing thrilling attractions such as "California Frank's Diving Horses" or "Mademoiselle Theresa and Professor Lola's Balloon Races" at the park. (A. Resnick)

Mike Mullins, c. 1908. Mike gives a hearty wave as he pulls his delivery cart through Bayonne. In 1905, the Census found 366 blacks in Bayonne. Many of them attended the Angelic Baptist Church on E. 46th Street. In 1906, John Tinker of W. 28th Street became the first black to hold a political position in Bayonne when Mayor Garven appointed him to a job at police headquarters. (Bayonne Public Library)

The groundbreaking ceremony for the high school on March 20, 1909. School board President James Benny turns the first shovel at this ceremony for Bayonne's new high school at the Boulevard and 31st Street. Trustees O. Farley, J. Murphy, and William Vreeland are present, as well as Principal P.H. Smith and Chief of Police John Yore. The building cost $265,000 and included a three-story gymnasium, as well as an elevator. (Bayonne Public Library)

A Wild West show, *c.* 1908. This cowboy manages to keep the flag in the air as he guides a calf around the green in front of the 8th Street station. He could be on his way to perform at Melville Park, which hired rodeo shows to perform each summer (see p. 86). (Bayonne Public Library)

Another *c.* 1908 photograph of a Wild West show. The boys on the right seem fascinated with this Sioux Indian in ceremonial dress bearing the Wild West banner on W. 8th Street. Sioux began joining rodeo shows after Buffalo Bill Cody persuaded Chief Sitting Bull to tour with him in 1885. (Bayonne Public Library)

With his dog standing happily beside him, this coachman drives a stagecoach from the Wild West show past the Mueller Brother's Cafe at 33 W. 8th Street. One of the new-fangled automobiles appears at the far end of the street. (Bayonne Public Library)

A police buggy, c. 1908. These patrolmen sit in their patrol wagon on W. 8th Street. At the start of the century, many barber shops offered "electrical massages" to stimulate hair growth, like the one advertised in Charles Grieco's barber shop in the background. (Bayonne Public Library)

Cheers, c. 1909. Joseph DiPietro (second from the left), the owner of this saloon on the corner of 23rd and Avenue C, stands proudly behind the bar, with Paul the bartender (left), Joseph La Palerma, and Gaetano Bombaggio (right). The other men in the photograph are, from left to right: (seated around the table) Vincenzo Maita, Joseph Macaluso, unknown, Nick Cutro, Nicola Alessi, and unknown; (lifting their glasses behind the table) Salvatore Panepinto, Carmen Esposito, unknown, unknown, Vito Vaccaro, Salvatore Militello, and unknown. (Bayonne Historical Society)

Anselmo Crisonino (1860–1918), c. 1909. As soon as Anselmo emigrated from Santo Menno, Italy, around 1890, he began saving money to bring his wife Elizabeth (1876–1964) to America. Within weeks of her arrival in 1900, they celebrated the birth of their first son, Amadeo ("Ed"). They saved their money and opened a restaurant on the Boulevard at 53rd Street. When a developer bought the property, Anselmo opened a shoemaker's shop at 898 Broadway. In their apartment upstairs, Elizabeth helped support the family by sewing for the movie studio next door (see p. 94). After Anselmo died during the great influenza epidemic (see p. 132), his sons Amadeo ("Ed") and Theodore ("Dido") ran the shoe-making business with help from their sister Beatrice and their brothers Dante, Louis, Galileo, and Anselmo. (Tina Mills)

Four
Hostilities at Home and Abroad
1910–1919

A flying boat, c. 1913. Before World War I, Bayonnites marveled at technological advances such as seaplanes, motorized cars, and moving pictures. This crowd gathers to watch a seaplane land in Newark Bay (see p. 104). It could be the one that landed at 27th Street in July 1913—the first plane to carry mail in the United States. To celebrate the event, the United States Postal Service held a two-day "hydroplane meet" on Newark Bay and issued a special cancellation stamp. (Bayonne Public Library)

Lincoln School, June 28, 1910. The boy in the front on the far right smiles impishly among these graduates holding their diplomas. Some of the graduates posing here are: Sarah Blair, Julia Fabula, Valentine Floytl, George Gadsby, James Glackin, Meyer Klein, Mary Kruger, Lavey Levine, Eileen Lindholm, Anna Lynch, Mary Price, Bessy Silk, and Clarence Woodruff.

A motor car outing, c. 1915. These young ladies gather for a picture in front of their new cars. Blanche Frankel kneels in the first row on the left. Cars rode on Bayonne's streets as early as 1904 when John Garnier became the first resident killed in a car accident. They were not widely popular, though, until after 1910. In 1912, Alfred Nann opened Bayonne's first car dealership, and by 1914, the city had four car repair shops to keep them all running.

Left: Hannah and Lewis Davis, *c.* 1910. After emigrating from eastern Europe in the 1870s, the Davises settled in Bayonne. Their son Frank became a photographer and eventually opened Davis Studios. (J. O'Donnell)

Right: Keep your eye on the ball, *c.* 1910. Nipper lifts his paw in applause for the man doing tricks with a small ball. (Bayonne Public Library)

Confirmation and First Communion group, June 1911. These young ladies of St. Vincent's Church pose outside the rectory on Avenue C at 47th Street after making their Confirmation and First Communion. Their sponsor, Miss Mary Cannon, stands in the back row to the right. (D. Cash)

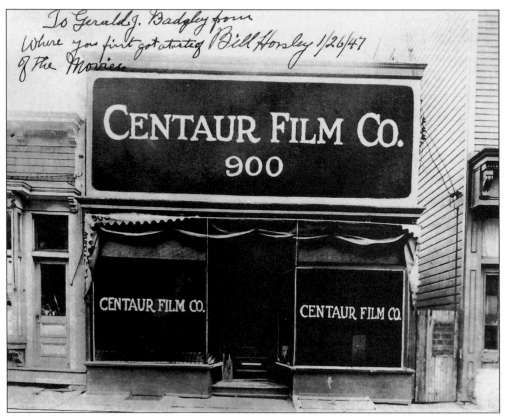

To Gerald J. Badgley from / Where you first got started Bill Horsley 1/26/47 / of the Movies

CENTAUR FILM CO.
900

CENTAUR FILM CO.   CENTAUR FILM CO.

The Centaur Film Company. When David Horsley's pool hall at 900 Broadway began losing money, he decided to turn it into a movie studio. In 1907, David and Charles Gorman, a New York scenic artist, created the Centaur Film Company—the first independent movie studio in America. Since neither David nor Charles had enough money to pay the patent fee for Thomas Edison's equipment, David built a camera out of some old telescopes in his father-in-law's basement. This make-do approach became the company's standard operating procedure. For their cowboy films, they used the woods on 54th Street as a set (see p. 57). For other scenes, they built sets in the backyard of 900 Broadway. For actors, they turned to the streets of Bayonne. Beatrice Crisonino Mills (b. 1909), who lived next door, recalls getting a surprise role in a gangster film. As she toddled down Broadway, two men in suits lifted her off the ground, threw her in a car, and raced away. Her father, watching from his shoe store (see p. 90), was not amused with David's improvisatory style. The new "Motion Picture Patents Company," a trust controlling the industry, was not either. When David applied for a license from the company, the executives who inspected his studio laughed at his homemade equipment and denied his license, forcing him to make movies independently. After two years of such shenanigans Charles Gorman sold his interest in Centaur to David's brother William. The Horsleys renamed it the Nestor Film Company, and by 1911 their films were grossing thousands a week. As the business grew, David decided to move it to California. Filming in Bayonne was difficult, because the vibrations from trains roaring through the city jarred the cameras (see p. 44). In addition, Bayonne's cold winters stopped the company from filming for several months each year. In October 1911 David moved the company to a small California town, Hollywood, where he opened a studio in a roadhouse that he rented for $30 a month. Other film makers soon joined him; today, CBS Television stands on the site of the roadhouse. (Gerald Badgley Collection, Library of Congress)

In the Commissioned Ranks, March 1911. Nestor sent programs like this one to theaters across the country to advertise its films. David Horsley's wife, May, recalled that most of the "props" for these early movies were taken from their home at 89 W. 41st Street. She always wondered what the neighbors thought as they saw the furniture being dragged in and out of the house. (Bebe Bergsten, the Nieber Collection)

NESTOR FILMS

Release of Wednesday, March 8, 1911

"IN THE COMMISSIONED RANKS"

Scene from "IN THE COMMISSIONED RANKS"

Order Now!   Don't Miss It!

DAVID HORSLEY, 147 Fourth Ave., New York

Desperate Desmond Almost Succeeds, 1911. David Horsley sits in the center of this poster for the first of Nestor's Desperate Desmond series, written by Harry Hershfield (standing, left), a cartoonist from *The New York Journal*. Harry developed the series as a spoof on nineteenth-century melodramas with the villainous "Desperate Desmond" battling the brave "Claude Eclaire" (played by Fred Kelsey) for the hand of the "Beautiful Rosamond" (played by Dorothy Davenport). (Marc Wanamaker, Bison Archives)

Taking office, January 1, 1912. Well-wishers sent these flowers to the council chambers at city hall to celebrate the inauguration of Mayor Matthew T. Cronin (seated, center) and the new city council. The councilmen standing here are John J. Boyle (far left), Edward F. Carbin, Daniel A. Dooley, John F. Driscoll, Benjamin F. Moser, Cornelius O'Mahoney, and Albert H. Phillips. (Bayonne Public Library)

The Oak Street fire, June 10, 1912. After a fire on June 9 destroyed six homes on Linnet Street, these Bayonnites gathered to see the damages. In the midst of the crowd, several men load what remains of the furniture from the house on the right into a wagon. The fire began after a spark from passing train set the wood in Booth's Lumberyard at Oak and Linnet Streets aflame. (Bayonne Public Library)

As Fire Chief Alfred Davis (center) inspects the damage on Linnet Street from the Oak Street fire, these boys admire his new red and polished brass car. Assistant Chief Louis S. Bonney leans on the door, while driver Thomas Pryor waits in the car. The Ford Motor Company built several of these Model T Torpedo Runabouts, fully equipped with fire bells and fire extinguishers, especially for fire chiefs. (Bayonne Public Library)

A toast, c. 1910. In their fashionable lace blouses and long narrow skirts, these ladies lift their punch glasses to toast Dr. Emanuel Klein (center). After graduating from medical school, Emanuel began his practice at Bayonne Hospital (see p. 134). In July 1914 he was appointed city physician by Mayor Albert ("Bert") J. Daly.

The Horace Mann School, December 1912. Having written their Christmas greeting on the blackboard, this first grade class poses around the Christmas tree in their classroom. While the children in the front solemnly hold the American flag in their laps, the others sit politely with their hands folded. (Bayonne Public Library)

Deliveries, May 1914. This boy stands on Broadway at 15th Street watching a man unload the delivery wagon on the left. Looking south on Broadway, one automobile appears in the distance near the railroad bridge. Even in 1914, most businesses used horse-drawn wagons for deliveries (see p. 102). (Bayonne Public Library)

The 8th Street green, May 1914. These boys pose on the green in front of the 8th Street station (right). After the photograph, they could have crossed the street for a sandwich at the Early Lunch Delicatessen, or for a game at Mueller Brother's Imperial Bowling Alley. (Bayonne Public Library)

St. Mary's School, 1912. With her arms crossed, Rose Sweeny Strauch (1896–1986) sits in the front row, third from the left, in this class picture (see p. 143). Like most of her classmates, she seems decidedly unhappy with the photo session outside the brick school on Avenue C at 14th Street. (M. McGlynn)

The YMCA, *c.* 1916. As in the other "factories" in Bayonne, the workers in this packaging plant trained diligently in order to produce quality goods: day after day, they toiled on the squash court, labored in the swimming pool, battled at the bowling lanes, and struggled at the rifle ranges within this building. One can only hope that they toiled not in vain. (Bayonne YMCA)

A gymnastics team, 1913. The boys who contorted themselves into this human pyramid were members of the first school gymnastics team. They practised four times a week with their coach, Mr. Samuel Belinkoff (right). Since only freshmen and sophmores were required to take gym class, Samuel probably formed the team to encourage juniors and seniors to exercise. (D. Cash)

The Bayonne High School Orchestra, 1913. The school orchestra began in 1908, when Mr. Charles S. Havens organized a group to play at the school's Friday morning assemblies, as well as the school's plays and musicales. By 1911, Miss Josephine G. Duke became the orchestra director, and Miss Lillian A. Clemons, a chemistry teacher, served as the orchestra's accompanist. Miss Duke stands here at the center with Mr. Havens to her right. The first violinists are Joseph Drissel, Bernard Dubinsky, Theodore Grotsky, Charlotte Herman, Rose Herman, Nathan Kantor, Benjamin Levy, Roy Mazzola, Joseph McCormack, and Martha McGinnis. The second violins are Samuel Appel, Leo Aronowitz, Ronald Bevan, Irving Boorstein, Gilbert Burn, John Guilfoyle, Charles S. Havens, Benjamin Hockstein, Walter Niedzialkowski, Gertrude Schaaf, William Sees, Edwin Troeller, Ruth Van Buskirk, and Frank Worman. The three students with the mandolins are Charlotte Hadlich, Joseph Scala, and Thomas Scala. In 1914, Miss Duke expanded the orchestra by adding a double bass, two drums, a cello, cornets, and a trombone. She also began rehearsing a band to play at athletic events. (D. Cash)

Resnick's Hardware Store, June 1912. Harry Resnick poses proudly in the doorway of his new store on Avenue E near 19th Street. The sign in the window on the left advertises "$2.50 IN GOODS FREE" with Merchants Home Stamps. Most hardware stores still sell "crockery" such as the jugs, pots, and pans on display in the window on the right. (A. Resnick)

Friedberg Mineral Waters, c. 1913. These three men pose with B. Friedberg's new motorized truck, loaded with bottles of mineral water. Beverage companies like B. Friedberg's were among the first businesses in the city to begin replacing horse-drawn wagons with trucks. Since bottles often broke during bumpy wagon rides, trucks ultimately saved these companies money. (R. Capriola)

Wigdor's Jewelry Store, c. 1914. Isaac Wigdor poses beneath the Gatsby-esque eyes on the sign outside his store at 446 Broadway. After hearing of Isaac's watchmaking skills, the Jersey Central Railroad paid him to come to Bayonne from Russia in 1888 to make their watches (see p. 44). As the sign suggests, Isaac was an optician as well as a jeweler. (Joseph Wigdor)

Resnick's Hardware Store, April 1916. Harry Resnick moved his hardware store to this building at the corner of Avenue C and 19th Street in 1913 (see opposite). He poses here during a sale he held before remodeling the building. The boy on the left stands in front of David Zeik's grocery store at 433 Avenue C. (A. Resnick)

A seaplane, *c.* 1913. As this seaplane floats in Newark Bay, three men check its right wing. Between 1913 and 1920, both the United States' Postal Service and Navy landed a number of seaplanes in the bay (see p. 91). During the summer of 1918, the Standard Aircraft Corporation of Elizabeth used Newark Bay to test the Curtiss-designed seaplanes it built for anti-submarine patrol in World War I. After the war, so many pilots continued to test seaplanes in the bay that the City planned to build a landing dock or "seaplane base" on the bay at 17th Street. (Bayonne Public Library)

Water ballet, *c.* 1915. The women and children sunbathing on this rock in Newark Bay laugh as a man poses upside down (center). (Bayonne Public Library)

Taking a dip, c. 1915. This woman looks fondly down at the children she guides through the water in Newark Bay. (Bayonne Public Library)

The Pavonia Yacht Club, c. 1914. This gentleman poses on the porch of the club's headquarters, the Jacob R. Schuyler mansion on Newark Bay at W. 11th Street—today's Pavonia Court. The club began looking for a permanent headquarters soon after it moved from New York Bay (see p. 82) to the Coombs' mansion at W. 41st Street in 1908. Once it bought the Schuyler estate in 1913, the club added a dock and built parking areas like the one on the left. (Newark Public Library)

Edwards Court—A Health Resort.   BAYONNE, N. J.

"Edwards Court—A Health Resort," c. 1915. As the caption on this postcard suggests, this street seemed like a resort in 1915, for right at the end of the block it offered swimming and fishing in Newark Bay. After Edwards Schuyler built the first home on this street in the nineteenth century, the road leading from Avenue A to his house became known as "Edwards Court." (A. Resnick)

Floating in Newark Bay, c. 1915. These women and children pose on a float in Newark Bay near Edwards Court. Women wore these cloth bathing caps and long bathing dresses until the 1930s. (Bayonne Public Library)

A parade, *c.* 1915. The girl with the pigtail on the right stood on the steps of St. Andrew's Chapel and School to watch the police lead this parade down W. 5th Street. Across the street, several sisters of St. Joseph watch the parade from the windows of their convent. (Bayonne Public Library)

Another view of a *c.* 1915 parade. Groups of girls in white dresses wave American flags as they follow this marching band west on 5th Street. The scene probably shows one of Bayonne's annual Sunday school parades in which children throughout Bayonne marched from their churches to the park at 19th Street. (Bayonne Public Library)

The Schwarzenbach-Huber Company, 1914. At the base of the utility pole on the right, two chickens seem to be grabbing lunch. The two men watching them stand outside the Schwarzenbach-Huber Silk Mill on Avenue E between 17th and 18th Streets. After Schwarzenbach-Huber took over the site in 1902, it expanded the building until it had 600 looms twisting silk fibers into fabric here. In 1925, the new Maiden Form Company moved to this site (see p. 157). (Bayonne Public Library)

Left: Helen Dzamba, c. 1910.
Right: Elizabeth Viroshi, c. 1910.
Like the women on the opposite page, Helen and Elizabeth were among the 600 workers who ran the looms at the Schwarzenbach-Huber Silk Mill (see above). If the lace work on their blouses is any guide, they must have been skilled seamstresses. (P. Gerard Nowicki)

Left: Julia Zec (Dietrich), c. 1915.
Right: Anna Dudash (Zec), c. 1915.
Julia's wide-brim hat and fur-trimmed cape were popular women's fashions around 1915, as were Anna's upswept hair and three-quarter sleeves. (P. Gerard Nowicki)

Left: Bertha Govrun, c. 1915.
Right: Anna Golias, c. 1915.
Anna and Bertha earned $2 per week, plus 1¢ for each yard of fabric that they finished, as did all the silk mill workers. (P. Gerard Nowicki)

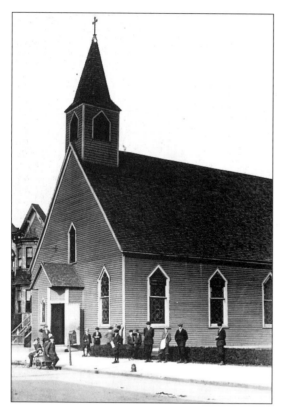

St. Henry's, 1914. These newsboys stand with their friends on Broadway near 26th Street, in front of the first St. Henry's Roman Catholic Church. Several German families who lived in this neighborhood began raising money to build a church in 1889. Since they needed a church immediately but had little money, they decided to design this wooden building so that they could use it as a school after they had built a stone church nearby. On Memorial Day, 1915, the parish finally dedicated its new stone church on Avenue C and 28th Street, one of the finest examples of English Gothic architecture in New Jersey. (Bayonne Public Library)

Mikado, May 18, 1914. When these students from St. Vincent's School performed this Gilbert and Sullivan operetta at the Lyceum Theater at 826 Broadway, James Moran starred as "Nanki-Poo" and Molly Brady played "Yum-Yum." Father Mark J. Duffy sits in the center, next to Frank B. Reed (left), a member of the original cast who helped rehearse the students. (D. Cash)

She Stoops to Conquer, February 20, 1914. Bayonne High School put on this production of Oliver Goldsmith's play with William Stillwell and Dorothy Van Winkle playing "Mr. and Mrs. Hardcastle." Some of the other cast members here are Frank Cleary, Ethel Davis, Fanny Feinburg, Meyer Klein, Lavey Levine, and Dorothy Van Winkle.

The Opera House, May 1914. In its newspaper advertisements, the Opera House hailed the photo-play on this marquis, *The Count of Monte Cristo*, as the "dramatic triumph of three decades." Like most photo-plays, *The Count* was shown in parts over three days. To see the whole movie, patrons had to buy three 10¢ tickets at this theater on Avenue C near 26th Street. (Bayonne Public Library)

The Centaur film-developing laboratory, 1915. After moving to Hollywood and forming the Universal Film Manufacturing Company, David Horsley returned to Bayonne in 1913, revived the old "Centaur" name, and opened a production center on Avenue E (see p. 94 and opposite). This photograph shows a clerk rolling film from the laboratory to the joining room in the production center (see p. 114). The man examining developing fluids by the window could be John Nicholas, a laboratory expert who ran this department for Centaur. Thomas Harding also worked here before becoming a cameraman in Hollywood. David initially used this building just to process the movies he made in Hollywood. Within a year, though, this center began processing film from Centaur cameramen around the world. In April 1914, David sent Al Seigler to film the USS *North*'s trip through the Gulf of Mexico. After processing the film in Bayonne, David sent a free copy of the movie to the US Navy for a review. Later in 1914, David opened a studio at 670 Avenue E for his new "Mutual Masterpiece" features (see opposite). One can easily imagine a young Charles Feldman (see p. 130) coming to the studio after school to watch the filming. In 1915, David decided to move back to Hollywood after he bought Frank T. Bostock's wild animal show while travelling with his wife May in England. He shipped the animals from England to Hollywood and opened a zoo, Horsley Park, at Main and 18th Street. He used the animals in a number of movies, which were all shipped back to Bayonne for processing. A press release in June 1915, announced that Centaur would be hiring people to process these films. For the next few years, David's various businesses boomed. After World War I began, however, David's zoo began losing money. The elephants, lions, and other animals cost a fortune to feed and maintain. To raise money, he sold his buildings in Bayonne to the Cello Film Company and the Universal Film Company. David left the film business in 1919, but members of his family continued to make pictures for the next sixty years. His brother William eventually opened a film laboratory on Sunset Boulevard, Hollywood, where he processed many of Walt Disney's early films. David's brother-in-law, Allen Davey, worked as a cameraman on such classics as *The Wizard of Oz*. David's son, David Stanley, worked as a cameraman on films such as *Francis the Talking Mule* and *Ben Hur*, and as a special effects man for films such as *The Bride of Frankenstein*. (Marc Wanamaker, Bison Archives)

Centaur Studio, 1915. The workmen on the left watch one of the scene painters finish a backdrop of a city skyline in a Centaur studio. By 1915, Centaur had earned enough money so that Milton Broeck, the property man, could buy "props" for the sets rather than borrow them from the Horsleys (see p. 95). (Marc Wanamaker, Bison Archives)

The Centaur Film building, 1915. David Horsley used this building at 686–88 Avenue E as a production center to process the movies he filmed throughout the world (see opposite). Four years after David sold this building to the Cello Film Company in 1917, a spark set one of the bailing machines ablaze. Ethel Suckow died in the flames, and Arthur Post, also caught in the blaze, died a few days later. (Marc Wanamaker, Bison Archives)

The Centaur positive joining room, 1915. Under these high intensity bulbs, Centaur employees joined various pieces of film together using equipment that David Horsley designed. David's sister-in-law, Ethel Davey, oversaw most of the editing work here. For *The Protest* (1915), she cut and spliced over 10,000 feet of film into the final 3,000-foot film. (Marc Wanamaker, Bison Archives)

The Centaur film shipping room, 1915. The boy in the center wheels a crate marked "C. Film, Bayonne" across the room, while various other clerks check invoices and pack film. From the shipping room, the films were sent to theaters across the country. (Marc Wanamaker, Bison Archives)

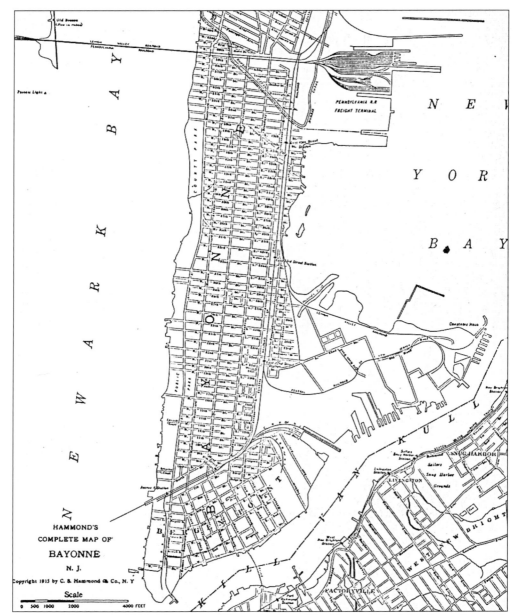

A map of Bayonne, 1915. This map of Bayonne from *The Hammond's Atlas* shows the city's modern street names (see p. 20), as well as its plans for the new County Park (see p. 149). (Bayonne Public Library)

The Standard Oil Strike of 1915, on July 21, 1915. As a crowd of strikers gathers in the distance, these shopkeepers huddle nervously along E. 22nd Street between Prospect Avenue and Avenue F on Constable Hook; a battle between the strikers and the Bayonne police earlier in the day had left one man dead. The battle was the first of many during the strike, which had begun on July 15 when one hundred still-cleaners at Standard Oil decided to ask for a fifteen percent pay increase. For $1.75 a day, they suffered through temperatures as hot as 150 degrees to clean out the sludge from the oil in the stills (see p. 31). After George Hennessey, Standard Oil's superintendent, refused to discuss their demands, the still-cleaners decided to go on strike. For two days, they picketed outside Standard's plant on the Hook. On Thursday the 17th, the strike became violent when a group of strikers confronted Antony Jozwicki, a Standard foreman, as he walked home from work. When Antony refused to join the strike, the mob attacked him. Standard closed the plant, putting 6,000 men out of work, to avoid further violence. Standard then directed Pearl Bergoff to find them armed "finks," (or strikebreakers), to protect the empty plant. Pearl had moved to Bayonne in 1909 after making a fortune using armed guards to break strikes. His men arrived on the evening of Tuesday, July 20, by the light of a tank fire, presumedly set by the strikers. Wednesday morning, the finks began work by starting a riot when they rushed onto E. 22nd Street to stop the strikers from picketing. The strikers stoned them, sending them running into Engine Co. No. 4's firehouse for protection. When Police Inspector Dan Cady came to stop the riot around 9 a.m., the strikers shot his horse. Dan shot into the crowd; John Stovanchik fell dead. After running into the firehouse for cover, Dan decided to hide in an ambulance on its way to Bayonne Hospital to escape the crowd. Yet as the ambulance pulled out of the firehouse, the strikers saw Dan crouched inside and began stoning it. The ambulance sped away in a shower of stones and bullets. The strikers then rolled these pipes into 22nd Street to keep other cars out of the area. The only vehicle they let pass down the street was the delivery wagon from Louis Cohn's grocery, parked here in front of Morris Edelstein's tailor shop. (Newark Public Library)

The battle at the Tidewater wall, July 22, 1915. Soon after this crowd began hurling rocks over the Tidewater wall, gunfire broke out leaving two dead and seven wounded. This battle was the second of the day. The first had begun further east on 22nd Street in front of the Standard plant. Just before 9 am, a striker threw a lit torch into a Standard building on the corner of E. 22nd Street and Avenue J. Though it burned itself out after a half-hour, the fire must have terrified the finks trapped behind the walls of the plant. While the flames grew, one of the finks shot Tony Bedlarski, age twenty-one, as he walked unarmed outside the Standard's wall on E. 22nd Street. Two hundred strikers standing across the street watched Tony fall, then stood quietly for a few minutes, stunned. Suddenly, Polish army veteran John Surgeon cried out and led the strikers across the street to hurl rocks at the finks. As bullets flew from behind the wall, John and Stephen Svahli fell wounded. The melee finally ended when Sheriff Eugene F. Kinkaid arrived at the scene and ordered the finks to stop shooting. He persuaded the strikers to go home by assuring them that the federal government was sending two mediators to force Standard to negotiate. Bayonne's mayor had asked Kinkaid, a former congressman, to take charge of the strike after the battle between the strikers and the Bayonne police the previous day (see opposite). After the sheriff stopped this first battle, the streets of the Hook remained quiet until these seventy-five boys began gathering in front of the Tidewater wall on E. 22nd Street near Avenue F. As this picture shows, a crowd of strikers soon joined the boys to throw rocks over the wall at the finks. The finks responded by climbing onto the roof of a building behind this wall to fire their rifles into the crowd. Kinkaid again stopped the battle, but only temporarily. As he walked away, someone hurled a lit torch over the wall, and the finks began shooting again. By the time a downpour finally stopped the battle, Frank Talos, age twelve, and Steven Samarek, age thirteen, were wounded. Gieresko Woisyk, age twenty-five, was killed when a bullet pierced his heart, as was nineteen-year-old Mikotay Ewaski, who stood watching the battle from Mydosh's Cafe (see p. 120). (Newark Public Library)

East Twenty-Second Street on July 22, 1915. A *New York Times* reporter described this scene on Tuesday evening as a surreal circus. After two days of rioting had left four dead and scores wounded, hundreds of youngsters began wandering E. 22nd Street, laughing "at the reports of revolvers and rifles now and then." To capture this view, an Underwood and Underwood photographer stood on the railroad bridge over 22nd Street looking east toward the oil plants. The Day or Night Quick Lunch Wagon on the left stood at the corner of Prospect and E. 22nd Street. Just an hour or so before these children gathered, this corner was filled with a mob attacking twenty-one-year-old Henry Olson, a guard for Tidewater Oil. As Henry walked down E. 22nd Street on his way home from work, the wind blew open his coat, revealing a guard badge beneath it. Someone on the corner of Avenue F saw the badge and shouted "guard!" Henry raced into a hallway of one of the buildings to hide, but a mob of strikers followed him. They dragged him out of the building and up E. 22nd Street into Marschak's Pharmacy, the shop beneath the "Ex-Lax" sign on the left here. While David Roscoe, the store manager, stood helpless, the mob pulled Henry into the shop and decided to try him for the crimes of the finks over the last two days. The crowd outside shouted "Kill him!" and "Murderer!" while people inside began giving testimony in the makeshift courtroom. Once the jury found Henry guilty, the "judge" decided to send him onto the street for punishment. As Henry struggled, the mob pulled him out to the street where they began clubbing and kicking him. One man beat Henry's face and skull with a hammer. After several minutes, nine men from the County Boulevard Police sped up on motorcycles and fired their pistols over the mob. While the mob paused, startled by the shots, the officers grabbed Henry and rushed him to Bayonne Hospital. Later that evening, 750 men leaving work at the General Chemical Company put their time cards in their hats to identify themselves to the finks and the strikers. (Newark Public Library)

Kinkaid's deputies, July, 1915. These deputies stand guard with two Bayonne policemen in front of the gate at Tidewater Oil on E. 22nd Street near Avenue F. To identify themselves to the strikers and the finks, the deputies put these cards in their hats, which said, "Sherriff's Aid, For the Protection of Life and Property" (see p. 118). Sheriff Kinkaid deputized over seven hundred of these men to help the police keep order during the strike. They worked twenty-four hours a day, taking turns to sleep on cots in the courtroom at police headquarters (see p. 78). (Newark Public Library)

Taking refuge, July 23, 1915. As strikers gather in the distance in front of Standard's wall on E. 22nd Street, these men and boys take refuge behind the cars of the Lehigh Valley Railroad (see p. 115). (Newark Public Library)

A meeting of strikers in July 1915. These strikers gather around John Mydosh's Cafe at the corner of 21st Street and Avenue F, their headquarters during the twelve-day strike. Once federal mediators arrived on the Hook on July 23, the action of the strike shifted from rioting to negotiating. While the mediators met with Standard and the strikers on July 24 and 25, Sheriff Kinkaid patrolled the Hook with his deputies to keep order. He arrested several strikers on weapons charges and closed several saloons for serving liquor illegally. He closed Mydosh's on July 24 after officers found several weapons hidden in one of its back rooms. The next day, Kinkaid arrested Pearl Bergoff and thirty-two finks for "inciting to riot." On the evening of the 25th, the City allowed Mydosh's to reopen for a strike meeting. After listening to several speakers, including Kinkaid, the strikers voted to return to work and continue negotiating with Standard over their working conditions. At 4 am the next morning, the sheriff and his deputies began escorting the workers down E. 22nd Street to the plants. While the negotiations continued over the next two months, the U.S. Commission on Industrial Relations released a controversial report that concluded Standard Oil "pays wages too low to maintain a family." The commission blamed the riots on the finks whom Pearl Bergoff had "recruited from the scum and dregs" of New York City. The report raised objections from newspapers across the country, which labelled the commission a "pack of radicals." Nevertheless, Standard soon granted a ten percent pay increase for everyone but its paraffine workers (see p. 124). On September 3, Standard also announced it would grant everyone but the paraffine workers an eight-hour day. Tidewater and Vacuum Oil announced similar policies within days. (Newark Public Library)

A baby parade, October 1915. To restore good will after the 1915 Strike, Bayonne's industries decided to celebrate the workers of the city with an exposition, or carnival, that featured a labor union parade, a dance contest, and a baby parade. This granddaughter of Herman Klein rode in the baby parade in this carriage. The chrysanthemums and hydrangeas surrounding here were in the suffragette colors, yellow and white. Some of the other babies in the parade were Edwin Creswick, who appeared as a huge oil can, and Hazel Milden, who rode in a model submarine. Bessie Talbot appeared on a float as "Little Miss Bayonne." Each stripe in her dress represented a Bayonne industry, and each point on her gold crown held a picture of one of Bayonne's five commissioners.

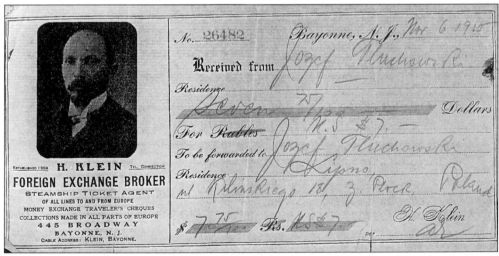

A receipt from H. Klein, November 6, 1915. Adolf Klein, Herman's son, gave this receipt to Jozef Fluchowski for $7.75 to be sent to Poland (see p. 42). Like many immigrant workers on the Hook, Jozef probably sent money back to Poland regularly. Even with the pay raises granted after the Strike of 1915, $7 would have been half of his weekly pay.

The Vreeland family, c. 1915. Joanna Vreeland poses with her sons William (left), Harry (seated), and Frank on the porch of their home at 74 W. 32nd Street (see p. 39). Until concrete became inexpensive later in the century, most people used wooden walkways like the one here. (Mrs. C.L. Vreeland)

The three brothers, c. 1915. William, Harry, and Frank Vreeland pose on the deck of their fishing and party boat as it stands docked at their boat house on Newark Bay at 32nd Street (see p. 51). On Thursday afternoons, Bayonnites waited here to buy whiting and blackfish from the brothers when they returned from their weekly fishing trips. (Mrs. C.L. Vreeland)

A good catch, *c*. 1915. Every weekend, the Vreeland brothers took passengers aboard the *Three Brothers* for fishing expeditions. Harry (left) and Frank pose here beside a passenger who seems pleased with his catch (see p. 153). Their boat is probably anchored in the Kill, given the oil tanks in the background. (Mrs. C.L. Vreeland)

A cruise, *c*. 1915. A man plays the banjo to entertain this group aboard the *Three Brothers* for a pleasure cruise. After stopping for lunch, the party would have headed back to the boat house on 32nd Street. (Mrs. C.L. Vreeland)

The special police, October 1916. These deputies march to duty on the Hook during the Standard Oil Strike of 1916. The 1916 strike began on Tuesday, October 4, when fifty paraffine workers stopped work to protest their low wages: $2.20 a day for unskilled workers and $3.20 a day for skilled workers. Unlike the other Standard employees, the paraffine workers had not received a raise after the 1915 Strike (see p. 120). On October 5, six hundred workers at Vacuum Oil joined the strike in sympathy with the paraffine workers. Standard workers from every department also met and voted to appoint a fifteen-man committee to voice their demands: a pay increase, an eight-hour work day for everyone, an unbiased system for firing, and a twenty- minute lunch (see p. 2). On October 9, Standard Superintendent George Hennessey rejected their demands, and 1,500 men from Standard decided to join the strike. The next morning, Standard's General Manager, George B. Gifford, announced that the strikers were all fired. He explained to a *Bayonne Times* reporter that he was "tired of these men going out on strike one day and coming back ready to eat grass a week later." While tensions grew, Bayonne's police followed a plan they developed after the Strike of 1915 and began forming a line down E. 22nd Street to separate the strikers from the armed guards within Standard and Tidewater Oil. On October 10, however, a riot broke out when the strikers rushed the police line. In the melee that followed, three patrolmen were shot and scores of strikers were injured. The following day, every plant on the Hook closed, putting 12,000 men out of work. Bayonne began swearing in seventy-five deputies to strengthen the police line on E. 22nd

Street. During the afternoon, 500 angry strikers marched to police headquarters to demand the release of three strikers arrested the previous day. Chief Michael Reilly, one of the only men left in the building, called the fire department for help, then raced to the front door. With his gun pointed in the air, he held the angry crowd at the door for fifteen minutes until one of their leaders persuaded them to go home. That evening, the whole Hook exploded as crowds of armed strikers rioted in the streets. The violence began around 7:30 pm on the 11th, with several hundred strikers setting the platform at the Lehigh Valley station ablaze. When firemen arrived to put out the fire, the strikers cut their fire hoses and began stoning them. After several policemen arrived and fired warning shots, the strikers went racing down E. 22nd Street. Meanwhile, another group of strikers set fire to a saloon on Avenue F, trapping Samuel Greenberg, his wife, and his daughter in their apartment on the second floor. With the police on the deadline and the firemen at the railway station, the fire burned out of control, forcing the Greenbergs onto the roof of the building. Detective Edward Griffin and his men finally heard about the blaze and brought ten firemen to the scene to rescue the Greenbergs. Around the corner at 100 E. 22nd Street, newly-wedded Sophie Torack watched the fires from the window of her second-floor apartment. When she saw the strikers running east from the Lehigh Valley station, she leaned out of the window to warn the firemen on Avenue F. As she screamed, a striker shot her in the head, and she fell onto E. 22nd Street. She died a few hours later. (Newark Public Library)

Looking for snipers, October 1916. After the violence on October 11, the Bayonne Police declared the Hook a "strike zone" and refused to let anyone either in or out of it. By the afternoon of October 13, armed strikers began shooting at the police from buildings and rooftops. To find the snipers, the police began random searches of men on the street, as well as raids on homes and businesses throughout the Hook. This picture from the Central News Photo Service shows a group of policemen standing guard while officers search a saloon for snipers. (Newark Public Library)

Strike duty, October 1916. These Bayonne policemen stand next to a building at the Tidewater Oil plant during the strike. While the police kept order from October 17–19, federal mediators held talks with the industries and the strikers. On October 19, the strikers voted to end the strike, and the next day everyone returned to work. Standard soon gave raises to all its employees and established a health and retirement plan for them. It also replaced Superintendent Hennessey and General Manager Gifford. (Newark Public Library)

First squad, 1916. These members of the Bayonne Police Department pose with Captain Noble Grigletter (right) on the side of their headquarters on Avenue C. They are, from left to right: (front row) E.M. Looby, J. Richards, M. Lautermilch, A. Angelowitz, C. Boos, D. Kilduff, J. Tierney, J. Lennon, P. Dowling, and E. Tierney; (back row) W. Troeller, T. McGrath, S. Harris, M. Donovan, J. Quinn, P. Gallagher, J. Moylan, P. Donovan, and J. Keegan. (Bayonne Police Department)

The General Chemical Company bowling team, 1917. Michael Ryan sits on the left with these fashionably dressed members of his bowling team. Like David Fable (center) and Patrick McNally (right) who stand behind him, Michael worked at the General Chemical Company, which began producing chemicals such as sulfuric acid and zinc chloride on the Hook in 1879. (Bayonne Public Library)

Alphonse Petti, c. 1917. Even though he would be leaving to fight in World War I within days, Alphonse poses calmly here in his army uniform. Like many Americans, he probably was not surprised when America entered the war on Good Friday, April 6, 1917. Since the beginning of the war in 1914, American ships had been repeatedly attacked by German submarines. In Bayonne, the mayor enlisted volunteers for a "home guard" to protect the city after the federal government blamed German spies for the Black Tom Explosion on the Lehigh Valley Railroad dock at Caven's Point, Jersey City—just blocks from Bayonne's city line (see p. 115). After America declared war in 1917, hundreds of Bayonne men between the ages of eighteen and forty-five registered for the draft. Company I was called into action in July (see p. 67). On September 21, the first 298 draftees were called into service. The next morning, they began marching to the 8th Street station to head for training at Camp Dix. (Bayonne Historical Society)

Leaving for war, September 22, 1917. The men holding their bags on the left pose outside the 8th Street station before joining the other 298 draftees leaving for Camp Dix (see above). By 9:00 am, over seven thousand people had gathered at the station to say goodbye to the soldiers. The sobs of the women on the platform were so loud that the train had to pull away from the station for roll call. (Bayonne Public Library)

Left: Corporal James J. Donovan, *c*. 1917.
Right: Sailor Charles Ryan, *c*. 1918.
James, a future mayor of Bayonne, received the Distinguished Service Medal and the Croix de Guerre for his heroism while serving with a medical detachment of the 312th Infantry. As a Navy diver, Charles helped plant mines in this waterproof suit and helmet. (Bayonne Historical Society)

Left: Edward and Walter J. Oleskie, *c*. 1917. Edward poses with his brother Walter, who at the age of seventeen ran off to Canada to enter the air force rather than wait a year to enter the American army. (B. James)
Right: Infantryman Samuel Jospey, *c*. 1917. Samuel fought in France in this uniform. (Bayonne Historical Society)

On the home front, 1918. While a cat checks their rear flank, Louis Gollin (left) and Donald Leigh pose in their uniforms with one of Herman Klein's granddaughters. The boys probably enjoyed watching the home guard drill behind the library (see p. 128), just a few blocks from their homes.

Charles Feldman (1905–1968), c. 1918. Charles proudly salutes in the Boy Scout uniform he wore to sell war bonds and hold clothing drives for the troops abroad. He had moved to Bayonne as a child when Mr. and Mrs. Samuel Feldman of 22nd Street adopted him after his parents' deaths. A few years after he graduated from Bayonne High, he went to law school in California where he became fascinated with David Horsely's Hollywood (see p. 94) while working as an assistant cameraman for John Ford. After graduating from law school, Charles opened an office in Hollywood and began using his legal skills to promote Hollywood stars. He served as an agent for John Wayne, Cary Cooper, Richard Burton, Greta Garbo, Kirk Douglas, and Marilyn Monroe, among others. He eventually began producing movies such as *The Seven Year Itch* and *The Group* to help his clients. In the 1950s, he risked his fortune to produce *The Glass Menagerie* and *A Streetcar Named Desire* by playwright Tennessee Williams.

Julia Zec (Dietrich), *c.* 1917. After the United States began daylight savings time to save energy during World War I, many Bayonne residents used the extra hour of evening light for walks in the park, as Julia (right) and her beau do here. Besides turning the clocks ahead one hour, Americans also saved energy by voluntarily keeping "heatless Mondays" throughout the brutal winters of 1917 and 1918. (P. Gerard Nowicki)

Home economics, *c.* 1918. In their kerchiefs and aprons, these students practice mixing ingredients in the cooking room at the high school. Like women across the country, they would have learned how to prepare special wartime recipes for wheatless "Victory bread" and sugarless cakes in order to save food for the troops. (Bayonne Public Library)

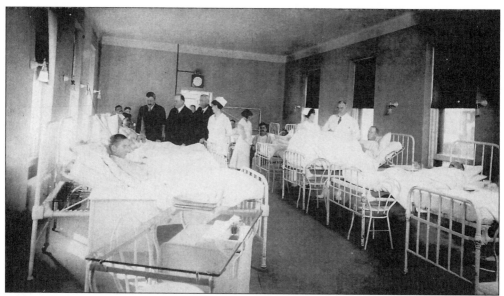

Daily rounds, c. 1918. These doctors and nurses check the patients in one of the men's wards at Bayonne Hospital. This staff worked bravely against the influenza epidemic that killed 22 million people worldwide between 1918 and 1922. In Bayonne, schools, churches, and other public buildings closed for weeks at a time to prevent the spread of the virus. (Bayonne Hospital)

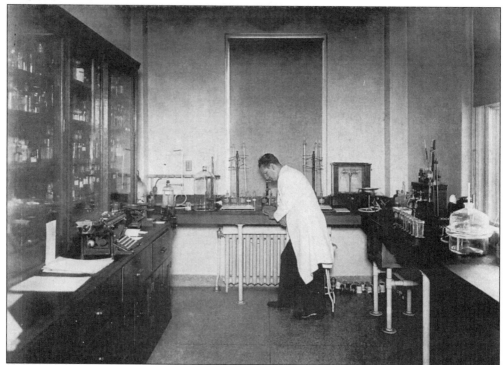

The pathology laboratory, c. 1918. Surrounded by bell-jars, scales, and chemicals, Dr. Morris Mans peers into the microscope in the pathology laboratory on the sixth floor of Bayonne Hospital. (Bayonne Hospital)

Traction, 1918. This child closes his fist as Supervising Nurse Grace Weidenham adjusts the weights attached to his feet. By keeping his feet in the air, the traction relieved the pressure on his fractured hip. (Bayonne Hospital)

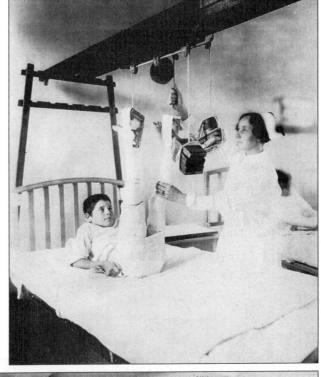

The children's ward, 1918. While the boy in traction smiles in the background, student nurses M. Martin and Bettie Sibbald wheel two children to the center of the room to hear a story from Supervising Nurse Grace Weidenham. (Bayonne Hospital)

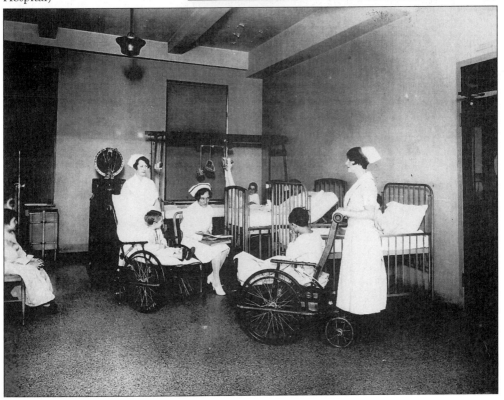

2nd Platoon B.F.D.

The Second Platoon of the Bayonne Fire Department, *c.* 1918. After modernizing the fire department with automobiles and motorized fire trucks, the City decided that it would be wiser to divide the men into two platoons that worked different shifts, rather than have all of them work twenty-three hour days. The First Platoon worked from 8 am to 6 pm, while the Second Platoon worked from 6 pm to 8 am. In the front row of this picture, S. Urbansky sits on the far left, Captain J. Bull sits fourth from the left, and Captain John Edmunds sits sixth from the left. The other captains in the front row are J. Corcoran, G. Crotty, V. Meyers, M. O'Keefe, and H. Sharrot. In the second row, the men in the white hats are, from left to right: Captain James Hogan, Director of Public Safety Henry Wilson, Fire Chief Alfred Davis, and Captain William McLaughlin. Standing at the far right of the third row is John Bauer. Some of the other firemen appointed to the second platoon were J. Bauer, H. Brown, J. Carner, J. Combes, C. Croney, G. Denny, C. Doyle, A. Feinberg, J. Friedman, W. Frick, D. Gallagher, J. Gibbons, R. Hartigan, A. Hendrickson, G. Hendrickson, T. Hogan, F. Keifer, J. Keating, A. Kupper, V. Laubenheimer, J. Lowrey, A. London, J. Lynch, A. Merkowski, J. Miller, J. Murray, J. Murphy, D. O'Neill, R. Quinn, J. Ryan, E. Rolzhausen, J. Sedik, H. Smith, L. Smeaton, T. Spence, J. Whalen, and J. Woodward. (Bayonne Fire Museum)

Civil War veterans, 1918. This portrait shows the fifteen remaining members of the Grand Army of the Republic, Post 155. Harry Turbert sits third from the left in the front row. Bayonne's Civil War veterans appeared in parades until the last two veterans, William Turbett and Michael J. Donnelly, died in the mid-1930s. (Bayonne Public Library)

Left: Anne Tucker, 1919.
Right: Nathan Tucker, 1919.
As soldiers began coming home after World War I ended on November 11, 1918, many young couples such as Nathan and Anne decided to get married. Anne's silk dress and underskirt was a popular post-war style for wedding dresses. (J. O'Donnell)

Welcome home, July 3, 1919. When Lieutenant-Colonel Dr. Lucius Donohoe returned from the war, ten thousand Bayonnites gathered at the 8th Street station to welcome him (see p. 101). John Nicholas Sacalis, of The Broadway Florist, poses here with some of the flowers residents ordered for the Lieutenant. The warm greeting must have consoled Lucius for his loss during the war; his wife Frances had died of the flu while serving with the Red Cross in England. (Bayonne Historical Society)

The Fourth of July, 1919. After World War I, Bayonne decided to hold a huge Fourth of July parade to honor its soldiers. These veterans march on Broadway. When they reached 33rd Street, two thousand school girls scattered flowers in front of them. In 1924, the City planted ninety-eight trees along Avenue B in memory of the ninety-eight men from Bayonne who died in the war.

Five
Between the Wars
1920–1940

Bayonne bridge, c. 1929. The steel girders of this 150-foot arch began stretching over the Kill Van Kull during the summer of 1929. Like the Empire State Building, which also opened in 1931, this bridge between Bayonne and Staten Island was an architectural marvel. At 1,675 feet, it was the longest arch span bridge in the world, a record it held until 1977 (see p. 151). (Bayonne Public Library)

Left: John Strauch, *c.* 1920. John takes a moment from his book to look at the camera. (M. McGlynn)

Right: Rose C. Rinaldi, *c.* 1920. Rose poses sweetly next to this wicker chair (see p. 158). (C. Karnoutsos)

Jazz band, *c.* 1923. Bill Powers, second from the left, blasts out the melody on the soprano saxophone during this rehearsal in a Bayonne living room. As the syncopated rhythms of jazz music began to spread from New Orleans in the 1920s, jazz bands began appearing in cities throughout the country. The hit songs of 1923 were "Yes, We Have No Bananas," "Barney Google," and "Tea For Two." (Bill James)

The Industrial "Y" staff, *c.* 1922. These maids, waiters, clerks, and boilermen were among the fifty employees who ran the YMCA on Avenue E at 22nd Street. Bayonne's industries spent nearly one million dollars to build this facility for their workers. The building was like a miniature city, with dormitory rooms for a hundred men, as well as a library, restaurant, soda fountain, barber shop, gymnasium, pool, and auditorium. Besides organizing athletic and cultural events for industrial workers, the Industrial "Y" also played a critical role in helping immigrants adjust to life in America, for it provided them with inexpensive housing while helping them become citizens and find jobs. (YMCA)

Strike!, *c.* 1922. This bowler seems to have nailed a strike in these lanes of the bowling alley at the "Y." Once the ball hit the pins, a "pinsetter" sitting behind the far wall would come out to reset them and roll back the ball. (YMCA)

A cabbage patch, *c.* 1925. These three boys hide among the cabbages at the Robinson Farm on Constable Hook. Even as late as 1925, Bayonne had three farmers: Al Green, Arthur H. Robinson, and William Smith. (L. Fahley)

Robinson's Farm, *c.* 1925. Arthur H. Robinson sowed these crops on his farm along Bayonne's northeast shore. The chimney of the American Radiator factory looms behind the homes on Fish's Lane in this view looking northeast. (L. Fahley)

Left: Farm chores, *c.* 1925. Arthur H. Robinson (left) and a farmhand pose with their pitchforks in front of a wagon of straw. (L. Fahley)
Right: Swimming, *c.* 1925. This detail from a larger photograph shows a crowd on the dock at the Bayswater Hotel at E. 43rd Street (see p. 83). (L. Fahley)

Spring planting, *c.* 1925. This horse waits patiently while Arthur H. Robinson tosses straw out of the wagon with a pitchfork. The farmhand would have then spread the straw over the field to keep the newly planted seeds from flying away in the wind. Behind the homes on the left lay Avenue E. (L. Fahley)

The Bayonne All Stars of 1922–23. This team played in a league at the Industrial "Y" (see p. 139). The members have been identified as Bart, Moloney, Findley, Wiengartner, Campbell, Mydosh, and Gleason. (Bayonne Public Library)

St. Vincent's, June 1924. When Father Joseph F. Dolan (center) returned to St. Vincent's in 1919, he quickly organized a school with help from the Sisters of St. Joseph from Philadelphia. Since the school building was not built until 1923, these twenty-nine students initially had classes in the church auditorium. Mary Heeney, Robert Reilly, and John Richardson are among the students holding their diplomas here. (Miss Cash)

Cross examination, c. 1923. Seated on the left in his robes, Judge Hyman Lazarus weighs the testimony during a trial in common pleas court (see p. 147). The witness seated on the right looks aggravated with the attorney's questions. (Bayonne Public Library)

The Nucoa Butter Company baseball team, June 14, 1924. This team portrait shows, from left to right: (front) Jim Paradine and Bobby Woods; (middle) Marion Gwynn, Bill Chambers, Charles Ryan, George Buchannan, Steve Freel, Leroy Wilson, and Walter Preston; (back) Al Crane, Frank Parenti, Al Brandt, Mr. Brundage, Wayne Marks, and Mike Ryan. (Bayonne Public Library)

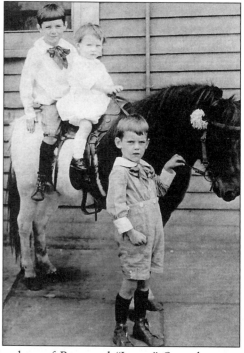

Rose Sweeny Strauch, c. 1930. Rose smiles happily as she poses in front of the apple tree in her fashionable cloche hat and side-buttoned coat. She and her husband "Lovey" (opposite) had four children: John (see p. 138), Marion (see below), Helen, and Delores Ann. (McGlynn Family)

Left: First communion, c. 1927. Marion, the daughter of Rose and "Lovey" Strauch, poses sweetly here in the white lace dress she wore for her first communion.
Right: Taking a ride, c. 1925. Joseph McGlynn leads his brothers Thomas (left) and John on a pony ride. Given Joe's sense of humor, one can only imagine where he took them. Several years later, Joseph wed Marion, and they had three children: Mary Rose, Thomas, and Joseph. (McGlynn Family)

Thomas Ludwig "Lovey" Strauch, *c.* 1925. In his leather jacket and work boots, "Lovey" confidently eyes the camera next to the tracks of the Jersey Central Railroad. The son of John and Honorah Strauch (see p. 58), "Lovey" began working for the railroad soon after he graduated from the Bayonne schools. (M. McGlynn)

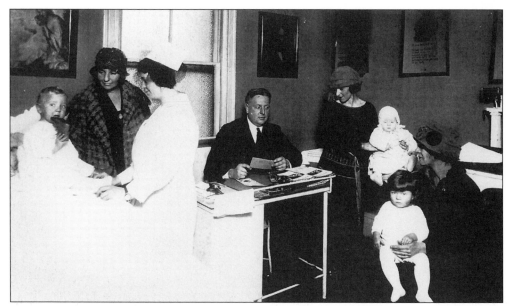

The Bayonne Clinic, 1928. The boy on the left nervously chews on a shoe as he waits for his treatment while the doctor (center) offers a prescription to the woman on the right. When it opened this clinic in 1928, Bayonne Hospital became one of the first hospitals in the country to offer outpatient services. (Bayonne Hospital)

The Junior Leaders Corp., 1928. William Hollenback (center) trained these young athletes at the Industrial "Y" (see p. 139). Standing from left to right are William Bierne, Henry Grodkiewicz, William Mitchell, Walter Organek, Charles Rutkowski, Ike Cohen, George Tenety, Stanley Jablonsky, Louis Bielinsky, Tom Koch, Stanley Kucinski, and Walter Pawlowski. (Bayonne Public Library)

The Crusaders, 1929. This champion team featured, from left to right: (front) Joe Bogueski, Steve Shanda, and George Romaine; (back) John Videtti, Henry Hornak, and Stanley Michanski. (Bayonne Public Library)

A track walker, August 3, 1928. This worker walks down Avenue C near 25th Street, banging the trolley rails back into shape with his sledgehammer. Next to the Opera House in the background stands the offices of *The Bayonne Times*, where S.I. Newhouse began his publishing career under Hyman Lazarus, the paper's owner and publisher. (Bayonne Public Library)

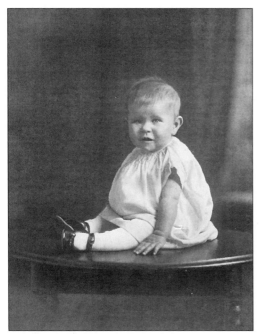

Left: Antoinette Dittrich, c. 1930. Antoinette sits cheerfully on the table in her embroidered dress and patent leather shoes. (P. Gerard Nowicki)
Right: The Zec brothers, c. 1930. Her cousins Andrew (left) and Paul (right) pose proudly with their brother Francis after he made his Holy Communion. (P. Gerard Nowicki)

Paster's, c. 1928. Samuel Paster opened this store in 1916. His wife Hattie stands next to the counter with their children Hannah (left), Gertrude (center), and Jack. Some of the signs in the store advertise Eastman Kodak film, Eversharp Pens, and Gem Razor Blades. A sign on the right offers cold cream for 25¢. (Bayonne Historical Society)

Hudson County Park, *c.* 1930. Looking east towards Avenue C, this view shows the fountains that ran down the center of W. 40th Street at the park's entrance (see p. 115). Since Hudson County opened this 52-acre park on Newark Bay in 1916, Bayonnites have come here to watch as the sun sets over the bay, to walk among the flower beds on its tree-lined paths, and to lower traps for crabs off its shores. (Bayonne Public Library)

"Hold; one, two . . ." In this *c.* 1932 photograph, these boys concentrate on holding their pose in the gymnasium at Bayonne Junior High School on Avenue A at 27th Street, built in 1926. Well into the 1960s, boys had to wear ties to school, and girls had to wear dresses. (Bayonne Public Library)

Cealus Van Buskirk (1866–1947), c. 1930. Cealus began wearing this uniform when he became an exempt fireman. He spent his life on W. 43rd Street, having been born in a house on Newark Bay that Nicholas Van Buskirk had given to his grandfather, who worked in the Van Buskirk's fisheries nearby. When Cealus wed Dora Jackson, they set up house on W. 43rd Street, and he began working on the Coomb's estate on W. 41st Street. Several years after Dora's death, Cealus wed Mary Thompson and began working at Tidewater Oil. (Bayonne Fire Department)

Bayonne bridge, c. 1929. The sides of the arch have almost joined in this view of the bridge from the Bayonne shore. After beginning the bridge in September 1928, the Port Authority of New York used 30,000 tons of steel to complete the arch and roadway. (Bayonne Public Library)

MOTOR HIGHWAY, PORT OF NEW YORK AUTHORITY BRIDGE, BAYONNE, N J

The Bayonne bridge on November 15, 1931. On opening day, 7,019 cars rode across the bridge after Edward Silk, a Bayonne contractor, became the first member of the public to drive across the span. WOR Radio carried the sounds of the opening day ceremonies around the country. The festivities included an eighteen-gun salute from the USS *Wickes* and the release of fifty carrier pigeons loaned by Captain James Gibbons, a Bayonne fireman. (Bayonne Public Library)

The 1st Street pier, August 1932. This scene, the left half of a larger photograph (see opposite), shows children playing in the sand next to the recreation pier that Bayonne opened on Newark Bay near 1st Street in 1932. With its large parking lot and beautiful view of the bay, the pier became a favorite site for picnics during the Depression. (Newark Public Library)

The Passaic Lighthouse, 1939. This lighthouse stood in Newark Bay off the shore of 51st Street, just south of the Lehigh Valley Railroad bridge in the background (see p. 115). The lighthouse's last keeper was Mrs. McCashin, a second-cousin of President William McKinley, who ran the light with her son after her husband died in 1912. Shortly after a photographer captured this view of the light, the government demolished it. (Newark Public Library)

The 1st Street pier, August 1932. A number of people enjoy swimming in the bay in this scene from a larger photograph (see opposite). The pier in the background created a pleasant beach by sheltering the shore from the swift currents near the Kill. The building at the far end of the pier held changing rooms and a lifeguard station. (Newark Public Library)

What a catch, 1934. Harry Vreeland (right) and his nephew Carl pose proudly with this sea-turtle that wandered into one of their nets in Newark Bay. After posing for the picture, they returned the turtle to the water. (C.L. Vreeland)

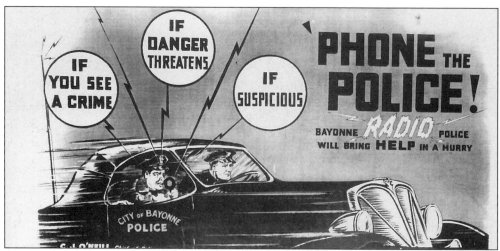

A radio poster, c. 1933. The Bayonne Police Department used this poster to advertise their new two-way radio cars, the first in the country to both receive and send radio messages. Thirty years later, the force was the first in the country to begin using walkie-talkies. (Bayonne Police)

Two-way radio cars, 1933. Director of Public Safety Jerome Brady (left) poses with Deputy Police Chief Dan Kilduff next to the new radio cars outside police headquarters on Avenue C near 26th Street. Motorcycle Patrolman Charles Nolan (left) and Patrolman John Boyle stand in the doorway. (Bayonne Police)

St. Henry's, 1935. Monseignor Mulligan (center) sits in a Dante chair among the graduating class of St. Henry's School. Edward Oleskie and Bill James have identified these students as, from left to right: (front row) Joe Hromack, Archie Bingham, Frank Herrmann, Aloysios McCarthy, Edward Brady, Tommy McDermott, and Tommy Brennan; (the girls sitting around Father in the second row) Gertrude Regan, Vera Long, Agnes Dee, Margaret Sharkey, Eileen Doyle, Betty O'Connor, Marie Limon, and Eileen McGlynn; (standing in the third row) George Wagner, William McGillis, Charles Devaney, Edward Oleskie, Edward Cody, Jack Leicht, Michael Reilly, Tommy Lenahan, Daniel Connell, unknown, unknown, and Harold Konzelman; (the girls in the fourth row) Marie Mahoney, Margie Doolan, Marion Cassidy, Mary Pavlik, Florence Kiernan, Rita Drexler, unknown, Ruth Cassidy, unknown, and Veronica McDermott; (standing in the back) Frank Matousek, Edward Masters, Edmond Mellendick, unknown, Eugene Jennings, John Bloom, Nelson Patnaude, Gerald Rochford, John McGeehan, and John Higgins. (Bill James)

A clown car, c. 1935. With their monkey friend perched on the back, these clowns take a drive to amuse the crowd at one of Babcock and Wilcox's annual field days. The company built the field for its fifteen hundred employees soon after it opened a boiler plant on the Kill between Hobart and Ingram Avenues in 1901. (Bayonne Historical Society)

The Standard Oil Glee Club, c. 1936. Edward Oleskie sits at the piano among the other singers and instrumentalists in this club. The group began during World War I when several men from the YMCA began visiting companies throughout Bayonne to lead workers in sing-a-longs. After they began rehearsing as the "S.O. Club" in February 1934, they performed around New Jersey. (Bill James)

Left: William and Ida Rosenthal, 1927. Several years after Russian emigrants William and Ida Rosenthal (left) opened a dress-making business with New York designer Enid Bisset, Ida designed and patented a new brassiere that gave women a natural appearance.

Right: The stretch test, c. 1938. A woman tests a piece of fabric in the Bayonne factory that the Rosenthals opened to produce Idas new product (see p. 108). (Maidenform)

Sewing operators, c. 1938. These seamstresses work in the Maidenform factory (see above). Jobs at Maidenform helped many Bayonne women support their families through the Great Depression of the 1930s. During World War II, Maidenform supported the war effort by producing "pigeon vests" to help soldiers transport their carrier pigeons safely. (Maidenform)

Left: Michael and Rose Ascolese, June 18, 1939. Michael and Rose race up Broadway near 19th Street to Robin's Studio for their wedding portrait. (C. Karnoutsos)
Right: The Herman Klein Travel Agency, *c.* 1926. Around 1910, Herman (center) moved his agency to this building at 445 Broadway (see p. 42).

Broadway, 1936. One of Bayonne's early buses travels south on Broadway past Nellie Gray Shoes and Valentine's Clothes Shop. Buses slowly replaced trolleys until, in 1938, Bayonne's last trolley car rolled through town. (Bayonne Public Library)

"The March of Bayonne," March 19, 1935. To mark Bayonne's 66th Anniversary, residents held a birthday party for the city at the junior high school (see below). In their glamorous satin dresses and tuxes, this group performed a comic radio sketch on Bayonne's history. Among the performers are George Allen, Edward Broad, Fray Fay, Edward Guterman, Marjorie Hahn, Reverend H. Lewis-Jones, Anson Lazarus, William O'Brien, Gladys Stalter, and George Stinson. (Bayonne Public Library)

"Sixty-niners," March 19, 1935. In the first six rows of this crowd celebrating Bayonne's 66th Anniversary sit the"sixty-niners," residents who had lived in Bayonne since its birth in 1869. Some of the early residents shown here on the left are Rose Brady, Mrs. Luther S. Cadugan, William Cubberly, William Hogan, Herman and Sarah Klein, Margaret Lee, Mrs. E. Russell, and Harry Vreeland. (Bayonne Public Library)

Select Bibliography

Harvey, Cornelius Burnham. *Genealogical History of Hudson and Bergen Counties, New Jersey.* New York: The New Jersey Genealogical Pub. Co., 1900.

Keenen, Edwina. *Bayonne Centennial Sketchbook: 1869–1969.* N.P.: n.p., 1969.

Levinson, Edward. *I Break Stikes: The Technique of Pearl L. Bergoff.* New York: R.M. McBride and Co., 1935.

Mandell, Paul. "David Horsley, Pioneer Picturemaker." *American Cinematographer* (March 1989): 44–52.

Nowicki, P. Gerard. "Movies were Movies." Unpublished essay, Bayonne Public Library.

Peacock, John. *Costume: 1066–1966.* London: Thames and Hudson, 1986.

Robinson, Walter F. *Bayonne Centennial Historical Revue: 1861–1961.* Progress Printing Co., 1961.

Shaw, William H. *History of Essex and Hudson Counties, New Jersey.* 2 vols. Philadelphia, 1884.

Sinclair, Gladys Mellor. *Bayonne Old and New: The City of Diversified Industry.* New York: Maranatha Pub., 1940.

Spehr, Paul C. *The Movies Begin; Making Movies in New Jersey.* Newark: The Newark Museum, 1977.

Winfield, Charles. *History of the County of Hudson, New Jersey From its Earliest Settlement to the Present Time.* New York: 1874.